NORMAN
GEISLER

FALSE
GODS
of OUR TIME

HARVEST HOUSE PUBLISHERS
Eugene, Oregon 97402

DEDICATION

I am grateful to Ronald Brooks
for his able assistance
in the preparation of this book.

FALSE GODS OF OUR TIME

Copyright © 1985 by Norman L. Geisler
Published by Harvest House Publishers
Eugene, Oregon 97402

Library of Congress Catalog Card Number 85-80486
ISBN 0-89081-495-5

Printed in the United States of America.

PREFACE

There was once a young man who worked in a state-owned building supply center in a Communist country. This young man was very clever, and the plant security staff was particularly careful to check him daily for smuggled building supplies, which could bring a good profit on the black market if they could be smuggled successfully out of the center. But the young man was very careful, and even though he was searched carefully every day, the guards could not catch him with any contraband.

The young man was doing extensive remodeling to his little farmhouse, and he was very careful to get written permission from the center manager to borrow a wheelbarrow to help him move the dirt he was excavating for a new basement at home.

Every afternoon the guards would stop him with the wheelbarrow at the gate. They would carefully search his clothes and lunch pail. Nothing. They would always demand his written permission for the wheelbarrow and then carefully examine the permission slip to be sure it was current and not forged. After nine months of being searched meticulously every day, the young man failed to show up for work one day.

No one knew where he was. The rumor went through the center that the young man had escaped to the West by bribing border guards with Western currency. No one knew how the young man could have afforded any bribe, much less bribes to several guards.

That evening on Western television news (which unfortunately did not broadcast to the young man's homeland and his coworkers and the guards) the young man, enjoying his first hours of freedom, was asked how he managed to escape from his country.

"Once I figured out how to do it, it was easy," he declared. "I knew the least dangerous escape, physically speaking, was to bribe the border guards. But I didn't have any money. If

I hadn't been able to smuggle 180 wheelbarrows out of my supply center and then sell them on the black market for Western currency, I never would have been able to afford it.''

This little story is amusing, but the point it makes is important: Sometimes, in spite of our diligence, the smuggling we are guarding against is going on right in front of us, and we don't even see it.

That is the thesis of this book: Atheism and pantheism are being smuggled into our society right under our noses, and many Christians are totally unaware of the secret danger which those two religious systems pose to Christianity. I have been a Christian and a professor of theology and apologetics* for almost 30 years, and I am convinced that the twin threats of atheism† and pantheism‡ are the biggest threats facing Christianity in America today. I am also convinced that unless Christians become aware of the danger and take positive steps to counter it, the wheelbarrows will have been sold on the black market while we are still examining the permission slips. This book§ will help you to become aware of the attack on Christianity being waged today by atheism and pantheism. More importantly, this book will show you how Christians, armed with the Word of God and the reason with which humans are endowed by their Creator, can withstand any attack against Christianity and successfully defend the gospel of Jesus Christ.

Norman L. Geisler, Ph.D.
Dallas, Texas
April 1985

---

* Apologetics is that branch of theology which states the reasons for accepting the Christian world view.
† Atheism means literally "without God," and is used here as the belief that no God(s) exist. The world is without, or at least does not need, God.
‡ Pantheism means literally "all is God" and identifies the whole world with God, making the world in some way part of God.
§ A companion six-tape video series is also available: Christianity Under Attack, distributed by Jeremiah Films, Burbank, California.

CONTENTS

CHAPTER 1

The Church Under Siege

The Christian church is under siege. From all sides Christianity is being attacked in the modern world. Atheism, under any of its aliases (such as "secular humanism"), and pantheism, whether religious or "secular," are the two biggest threats to Christianity.

The twentieth century has rightly been called the "secular century." The U.S.S.R. is the first large atheistic country known in human history. The leading Soviet government newspaper, *Izvestia* stated in October 1981, "Unfortunately, some of our people harbor the illusion that religion and its traditions are harmless. They forget that no matter what sophisticated forms religion may take in today's conditions, the essence of religion as an antiscientific world view remains the same. Religion hampers the development of man's creative and public activity" (quoted in *The Los Angeles Times*, May 16, 1982).

The Communist Chinese government has avidly promoted atheism, seeking to eradicate the Buddhistic and Christian beliefs of its people. Marxist regimes are often unstable governments, promising their people many things in the name of Marxism, but frequently unable to deliver. The tragic mass starvation rampant in Marxist-controlled Ethiopia is one example. Civil unrest in small South American and African countries is often funded and promoted by outside Communist agitators, who can promise freedom of religion under Communist rule, but who actually support the atheism of true Marxism.

And the "Christianized" Western world has not escaped this secularization either. Regular church attendance and belief in God has declined to such an extent that in some European countries fewer than half the citizens make religious activities a regular part of their lives.

Freeing America From Religion

The United States has also become a battleground for the battle between secularization and religion. The constitutional guarantee of freedom of religion has been reinterpreted over the last few decades into a guarantee of freedom *from* religion. The ACLU has consistently championed the rights of secular humanism against the rights of religion. Secular "human rights advocates" are arguing for the "rights" of the terminally ill to kill themselves and the "rights" of parents of multihandicapped newborns to starve their babies to death. The Supreme Court in 1973 gave every American woman the "right" to kill her unborn baby, with only a few ineffective restrictions. Public education in America has been secularized in a multitude of areas. Minors must obtain parental consent to get their ears pierced but can obtain contraceptives and even abortions without their parents' knowledge or consent. Schools have even allowed students out of class to obtain abortions and yet are not required to inform parents that their children were off campus!

Colleges and universities are not exempt from this secularized bias either. For example, Iowa State University has discussed the possibility of flunking students from science classes if they dare to espouse creationism, and has also discussed the possibility of retroactively taking away earned degrees from graduates who become scientific creationists! Iowa State University professor John W. Patterson stated, "I suggest that every professor should reserve the right to fail any student in his class, no matter what the grade record indicates, whenever basic misunderstandings of a certain magnitude are discovered. Moreover, I would propose retracting grades and possibly even degrees if such gross misunderstandings are publicly espoused after passing the course or after being graduated."[1] There have been several court suits lodged by teachers who say they have lost their jobs or been denied tenure because of their creationist views.

Eastern Enlightenment?

Another result of this antichristian trend has been a paradoxical "turn to the East." Millions of people, convinced by our postchristian society that Christianity is dead, have looked elsewhere for the spiritual fulfillment they so desperately need. They have looked to the East, to the philosophies and often the religions of Hinduism, Buddhism, Shinto, and Taoism. They have turned from the Christian God—the great "I AM," the Creator, distinct from His creation—to a pantheistic god, a god of whom it is said, "God is All and All is God," and which is one with creation itself.

The Popularity of Pantheism

Pantheism is now enjoying a popularity never before seen in the Western world. Popular pantheism* can be grouped into several different classifications. There is traditional religious pantheism, represented by the many religious cults imported

---

* Although pantheism can be classified philosophically as absolute, emanational, developmental, modal, multilevel, and permeational, all types of pantheism identify the world with God, making God in some way part of the world. Pantheists differ in how they explain this identity.

from the East, such as the Rajneeshees and the Ramakrishna
Vedanta Society. There is also modified religious pantheism,
represented by the many religious cults which have been modified in form to appeal to Western minds and culture, but which
still adhere to religious pantheism. Such cults as Transcendental
Meditation (TM) and Nichiren Shoshu Buddhism (Sokkagakai)
are "Westernized" Eastern imports. The third kind of popular pantheism in the United States is almost a marriage between
pantheism and atheism. It is represented by those movements
which appear to be nonreligious or even atheistic but which
build their whole systems on the belief that pantheism is true.
For example, est (Erhard Seminars Training) claims to be a
nonreligious, humanistic system to achieve success and
"self-actualization" through a secular pop-psychology
approach to self-help. However, est presupposes that the reason
you are unfulfilled is that you have forgotten that you are your
own God, and that the world around you is merely an extension of your mind. Fulfillment comes, according to est, when
you operate continually in the "reality" of your own divinity!

You do not need to be an expert in philosophy and religion
in order to understand the basic concepts outlined in this book.
As responsible Christians, we all need to know and understand
that pantheistic thought (whether religious or philosophical)
and atheism (whether militant or seemingly benign) stand in
direct opposition to the God who exists, the God of the Bible,
the eternal Creator and Sustainer of all things.

Atheism Attacks Christianity

One atheist organization, Atheists United of California,
clearly declares its active opposition to Christianity:

> Working with Atheists United means: You're
> demonstrating your freedom and backing it up with
> meaningful, concerted action. You're tired of sub-
> sidizing tax-free superstitions. You don't want
> your children and grandchildren to continue to be

indoctrinated with fairy tale mythologies. You want to be part of the fight against ignorance. You're ready to have some effect on the real world. As President Kennedy reminded us, the greatest evil is for good men to do nothing. Join the fight against religionists who want to force you to live by their medieval rules. It's moral, it's timely, and it's essential. We need YOU to join with us TODAY. Tomorrow may be too late![2]

The leading secular humanists of today together signed the Humanist Manifesto II, and it reads in part:

Though we consider the religious forms and ideas of our fathers no longer adequate, the quest for the good life is still the central task for mankind. Man is at last becoming aware that he alone is responsible for the realization of the world of his dreams, that he has within himself the power for its achievement. He must set intelligence and will to the task.[3]

Atheists in America are becoming more and more vigorous in their recruiting efforts. One atheist organization, the Freedom From Religion Foundation, has even formed a group called "Christians Anonymous," "a unique support service for persons who are recovering from religion-dependency. Just as Alcoholics Anonymous serves recovering alcoholics, so Christians Anonymous offers a helping hand to those persons who are rejecting religion. . . . The Foundation emphasizes that the support service is not just for unfortunates who may have become affiliated with cults, but for those persons connected with 'mainstream' religions—Catholic, Lutheran, Mormon, whatever."[4]

Pantheism Attacks Christianity

There is an even wider diversity of organization among the

many pantheistic movements and cults which are diametrically opposed to Christianity and the Bible.

For example, Bhagwan Shree ("Sir God") Rajneesh said of Christianity, "Not only is LSD a drug, Christianity is also, and a far more complex and subtle drug which gives you a sort of blindness. You cannot see what is happening, you cannot feel how you are wasting your life."[5] He also stated, "I don't want you to become Christians—that is useless, that is a lie."[6]

Werner Erhard's est directly attacks the biblical distinction between God and His creation, teaching instead, "...in the est training YOU are God.... Therefore, you cannot look to any supreme being for special treatment, goodness, or award."[7]

A Western brand of pantheism was developed in the early years of this century by a man named Edgar Cayce, whose Association for Research and Enlightenment carries on his work of promoting pantheism, reincarnation, and psychic phenomena. In *A Search for God, Book I,* the A.R.E. notes, "In the universe all manifestations are of God and are one with Him.... How wonderful to realize that there is only one force, one power, one presence, and that is God, the Father."[8]

Reviewing the Battle Plan

This book presents the battle against Christianity being waged today in America. By reading this book, the Christian reader will understand the threat posed by atheism and pantheism, will understand what different beliefs in God are possible, and will learn how Christianity can meet and beat any challenge presented by any alternate belief system.

In Chapter 2 we will survey different ideas about God which compete with the biblical revelation concerning God.

In Chapters 3 and 4 we will see how the biblical God is attacked by atheism, and then how the biblical God is attacked by pantheism.

An integral part of defending the biblical God and the biblical record concerning Jesus Christ against naturalism is a sound, objective defense of the possibility of the miraculous, and then a reasonable presentation of the biblical miracles. This is the subject of Chapter 5.

Chapters 6 and 7 will help us to see the insidious attacks of atheism and pantheism against the person and work of Jesus Christ. We will also develop a convincing argument in support of the biblical Jesus Christ.

In Chapter 8 we will review the biblical assurances that God and Christ are ultimately victorious over all challenges. We will discuss specific steps that you can take to combat the spread of atheism and pantheism in America today. You will learn that your commitment to God's Word, and your willingness to act on that commitment, will become a part of God's plan in fighting the inroads made by these two great threats to the Christian faith.

Meeting the Challenge

We have seen from this short survey that atheism and pantheism are on the attack against Christianity. Christians cannot afford to sit back and watch while these two forms of unbelief try to destroy Christianity. The Bible in numerous passages commands us to defend our faith, to stand up for the truth that is in Christ, and to combat false beliefs and false gods with the truth of the Word of God.

First Peter 3:15 commands, "Always be prepared to give an answer to everyone who asks you to give the reason for the hope that you have" (NIV).

The battle against Christianity is not just a battle on the human level; it is a spiritual battle between the forces of darkness and the God of light. Ephesians 6:10-13 both admonishes and encourages Christians concerning this spiritual battle:

> Finally, be strong in the Lord and in his mighty
> power. Put on the full armor of God so that you
> can take your stand against the devil's schemes. For
> our struggle is not against flesh and blood, but

against the rulers, against the authorities, against
the powers of this dark world and against the
spiritual forces of evil in the heavenly realms. Therefore put on the full armor of God, so that when the
day of evil comes, you may be able to stand your
ground, and after you have done everything, to stand
(NIV).

The apostle Paul was one of the greatest Christian
apologists—defenders of the faith—who has ever lived. Paul
did not stand by silently while nonbelievers ridiculed Christianity. Paul was a bold witness for the resurrected Christ,
ready at every moment to preach the gospel and defend the
faith. Numerous times in the New Testament his commitment
to truth is recorded, as in Acts 17:16,17:

While Paul was waiting for them in Athens, he
was greatly distressed to see that the city was full
of idols. So he reasoned in the synagogue with the
Jews and the God-fearing Greeks, as well as in the
marketplace day by day with those who happened
to be there (NIV).

God and Christ Victorious

You don't have to be a consummate Christian warrior to
be able to fight the battles for faith that you encounter in your
daily life. But each Christian has the obligation before Jesus
Christ to "contend for the faith that was once for all entrusted
to the saints" (Jude 3). Parents have this obligation toward
their children, who will face attacks in the public schools.
Professionals have this obligation to their personal integrity,
which will be tested repeatedly with self-deification offered in
various forms. Students have this obligation to their Christian commitment, which will be attacked repeatedly in the arena
of today's American educational system. Every Christian has

this obligation to his Lord and Savior, Jesus Christ, who declared, "I am the way and the truth and the life; no one comes to the Father except through me" (John 14:6 NIV).

Christianity is not a myth. It is not a figment of someone's overactive imagination. Christianity is not a dream world, separated from reality, nor is it the delusion of a madman.

On the contrary, Christianity is the only world view (way of looking at the world) which corresponds exactly, perfectly, and fully to reality. The claims of Jesus Christ can be tested, and those claims can easily be demonstrated as truthful by objective, reasonable tests rooted in reality. The same Jesus Christ who is God is the Jesus Christ of history, the Jesus Christ who died on the cross and rose from the dead with many convincing proofs (Acts 1:3).

Second Peter 1:16,19 should be our pledge as we set out to defend our faith:

> We did not follow cleverly invented stories when we told you about the power and coming of our Lord Jesus Christ, but we were eyewitnesses of his majesty. . . . And we have the word of the prophets made more certain, and you will do well to pay attention to it, as to a light shining in a dark place, until the day dawns and the morning star rises in your hearts (NIV).

CHAPTER 2

False Gods of Our Time

Don't be fooled: Even in our "secular" modern world, false gods are everywhere. Every single human being worships something. Not everyone worships or believes in a god or gods in the same way, but everyone worships something. Even atheists worship something, whether that something is themselves, the universe, or something else. That atheism can be religious was noted by the United States Supreme Court, which observed the following about several types of atheism: "Among religions in this country which do not teach what would generally be considered a belief in the existence of god are Buddhism, Taoism, Ethical Culture, Secular Humanism and others" (Torcaso, 1961).

Kinds of Belief in God

Evangelist Billy Graham has observed this same phenomenon: Everyone worships something. He notes:

> A remarkable fact for all seekers of God is that belief in some kind of God is practically universal. whatever period of history we study, whatever culture we examine, if we look back in time we see

all peoples, primitive or modern, acknowledging some kind of deity. . . .

Some people give up the pursuit of God in frustration, calling themselves "atheists" or "agnostics," professing to be irreligious. Instead they find it necessary to fill the vacuum left within them with some other kind of deity. Therefore man makes his own "god"—money, work, success, fame, sex, or alcohol, even food. . . .

Failing to find the true God, millions declare their allegiance to lesser gods and causes. They find no ultimate answers or satisfaction, however. Just as Adam was made for fellowship with God, so are all men. . . . Man, unlike a stone or an animal, has the capacity to love God.[1]

The following summary and chart will help you to visualize the possible "god options," or the possible categories of belief. Let's start at the beginning.

One either believes in some sort of god, or he doesn't. In other words, one either believes atheism or else has some belief in god(s). Much of this book will deal with atheistic and pantheistic beliefs, which I believe to be two of the greatest attacks on Christianity in modern society.

If one believes in some sort of god(s), he either believes in many gods (polytheism) or he believes in one god. Note that a polytheist could believe in just two gods or in any number greater than that. A polytheist may even believe in one big god and other smaller gods, a variation of polytheism sometimes known as henotheism.

If one believes in one god, then he either identifies that god with the universe (pantheism) or else he believes that god is distinct in essence* from the universe. The pantheist, for

—————————————————————————

* A simple working definition of essence as I am using it here would be "what makes a thing what it is, and not something else." God's essence is what makes him God and not anything else.

example, would not agree that God created the universe out of nothing but instead out of himself. A significant variation from pantheism is called panentheism, which identifies God with the universe in a very close but slightly differentiated way, somewhat like the relationship in man between the body and the soul.

CATEGORIES OF BELIEF

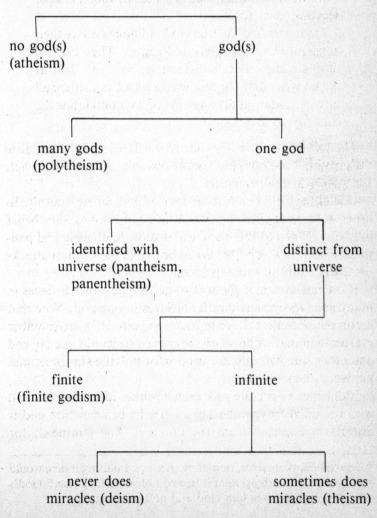

no god(s) (atheism)

god(s)

many gods (polytheism)

one god

identified with universe (pantheism, panentheism)

distinct from universe

finite (finite godism)

infinite

never does miracles (deism)

sometimes does miracles (theism)

If one believes that God is infinite, then he believes that God does or does not act in his creation, the universe. The belief that God does not act in his universe is called deism. The deist must deny all miracles: God does not perform miracles. The belief that this one God, distinct from his universe and infinite, *does* act in the universe is called theism. Christians are theists. (Judaism and Islam are also theistic.) We believe that God can and does act in our universe. We believe that miracles are possible.

Seven Basic Views

From this we can see logically that there are seven basic categories of belief about God: 1) atheism, 2) polytheism, 3) pantheism, 4) panentheism, 5) finite godism, 6) deism, and 7) theism. Each one of these views is mutually exclusive to the other six. This means that one cannot be consistent or non-contradictory and believe two of the seven views at one time.* For example, it would be contradictory to say that you believed that God is both finite and infinite. There are six false gods, or views of god, competing for the hearts and souls of people against the one true God, the God of the Bible.

In spite of this battle for the souls of people, many Christians are not aware of these false beliefs, do not understand what these false beliefs mean, and do not know how to combat such false beliefs. It is important to understand false belief and, more importantly, to be able to understand and communicate why the God of the Bible is the only true God. We will not discuss these seven views in the order given above, however. We will begin by presenting the true belief, theism, so that we have a standard by which we can compare all of the other beliefs.

---

* Some religious systems, asserting that contradiction and inconsistency are real, embrace more than one idea (such as Hinduism's pantheism and finite polytheism.)

Theism

Theism is the belief that one infinite God exists beyond but acts in the universe. Theism says that the physical universe is not all that exists. There is an infinite, personal God beyond the universe who created it, who sustains it, and who can act within it supernaturally. This is the belief held by Judaism, Christianity, and Islam. (However, as we shall see further in our discussion, these three religions have different beliefs about this one God.)

The theistic God is the God of Abraham, Isaac, and Jacob, as well as the God of Peter, Paul, and John. He is the God of the Bible. The theistic view of God has been upheld by all orthodox Christian teachers through the centuries, including the New Testament writers, the early church leaders, St. Augustine, St. Anselm, St. Thomas Aquinas, and such great Reformers as Luther, Calvin, and Swingli. There have been literally millions of Christians through church history who have affirmed belief in the one true God of the Bible. C. S. Lewis, a Christian scholar and professor of literature, was also a popular British writer, and his 1943 description of the theistic God remains clear and relevant today:

> God invented and made the universe—like a man making a picture or composing a tune. A painter is not a picture, and he does not die if his picture is destroyed. You may say, "He's put a lot of himself into it," but you only mean that all its beauty and interest has come out of his head. His skill is not in the picture in the same way that it is in his head, or even in his hands.[2]

God does not emerge from nature; rather, He transcends it, as Lewis also noted:

> The cosmic mind will help us only if we put it at the beginning, if we suppose it to be, not the product of the total system, but the basic, original,

self-existent Fact which exists in its own right. But to admit that sort of cosmic mind is to admit a God outside Nature, a transcendent and supernatural God.[3]

The God of the Bible* is the transcendent, eternal, infinite God. Genesis 1:1 tells us, "In the beginning God created the heavens and the earth." The book of Job describes God as the One who "laid the earth's foundation," "marked off its dimensions," "stretched a measuring line across it," and "laid its cornerstone" (Job 38:4-6 NIV). He is clearly the Creator, not the creation or part of it. Psalm 90:2 pays tribute to the eternal Lord: "Before the mountains were born or you brought forth the earth and the world, from everlasting to everlasting you are God" (NIV). The prophet Isaiah also recorded the words of the Lord, testimony to his creative power: "I am the Lord, who has made all things, who alone stretched out the heavens, who spread out the earth by myself" (Isaiah 44:24 NIV). The New Testament also gives eloquent testimony to the distinction between God and the creation. The apostle John acknowledges that the Word (Jesus Christ) is God, opening his Gospel (1:1-3) with the following words:

> In the beginning was the Word, and the Word was with God, and the Word was God. He was with God in the beginning. Through him all things were made; without him nothing was made that has been made (NIV).

In Acts 17 the apostle Paul challenged the Greek philosophers by declaring "The God who made the world and everything in it is the Lord of heaven and earth and does not live in temples built by hands. And he is not served by human

---

* I will not present here a defense for the inspiration and inerrancy of the Bible, which I have covered in other books. A basic introduction is a book I co-authored with William Nix, *A General Introduction to the Bible* (Chicago: Moody Press, 1968).

hands, as if he needed anything, because he himself gives all men life and breath and everything else" (v. 24-25 NIV). The New Testament book of Hebrews compares God creating the universe to man building: "For every house is built by some-one, but God is the builder of everything" (3:4 NIV). Even the very last book of the Bible, Revelation, declares the distinction between God and the universe, proclaiming, "You are worthy, our Lord and God, to receive glory and honor and power, for you created all things, and by your will they were created and have their being" (4:11 NIV).

From the above we can see clearly that the Bible is consis-tent from beginning to end, from Genesis to Revelation: There is an essential distinction between God, the eternal Creator, and the universe, which began through the creative agency of God. Furthermore, the Scriptures teach us that the universe continues to exist, or is sustained, by God. Acts 17:25,28 tell us, "He himself gives all men life and breath and everything else. . . . In him we live and move and have our being" (NIV). Colossians 1:17 adds, speaking of Jesus Christ as God, "He is before all things, and in him all things hold together" (NIV).

The difference between God existing and God not existing is an enormous one, affecting even our moral conscience, as C. S. Lewis noted:

> Does it not make a great difference whether I am,
> so to speak, the landlord of my own mind and body,
> or only a tenant, responsible to the real landlord?
> If somebody else made me, for his own purposes,
> then I shall have a lot of duties which I should not
> have if I simply belonged to myself.[4]

The psalmist put it this way: "It is he who has made us, and not we ourselves; we are his people, the sheep of his pasture" (Psalm 100:3 NIV). Compare this with the empty morality of an atheistic universe as presented by the popular host of Cosmos, astronomer Carl Sagan:

> . . .our obligation to survive is owed not just to

ourselves but also to that COSMOS, ancient and vast, from which we spring.[5] If we must worship a power greater than ourselves, does it not make sense to revere the sun and stars? Hidden within every astronomical investigation, sometimes so deeply buried that the researcher himself is unaware of its presence, lies a kernel of awe.[6]

There is a Creator; he is eternal, infinite, and distinct from his creation; and we, as his creation, belong to him and are morally obligated to him.

In stark contrast to this Christian view of God (theism or monotheism), there are many nonchristian gods marching across the stage of the contemporary world. We will now survey the six alternate views we listed and defined above.

Atheism

Atheism is the belief* that no God exists beyond the universe or in it. Atheism says that the universe is all there is. No God exists anywhere, at any time. As Carl Sagan says:

> The cosmos is all that is
> or ever was
> or ever will be.[7]

The universe is self-sustaining. For example, the "father" of evolution, Charles Darwin, replaced the Creator of all living things with "natural selection," his theory of the natural origin of the species: "I speak of natural selection as an active power or deity; but who objects to an author speaking of the attraction of gravity as ruling the movements of the planets...."[8] Popular atheist author Ayn Rand declared, "Matter is indestructible, it changes its forms, but it cannot cease to exist."[9]

---

* Evidence is presented in this chapter to affirm that atheism is active belief and not merely absence of belief, as some atheists try to assert.

   Philosopher Paul Kurtz, one of America's most well-known secular humanists, echoed this thought in the *Humanist Manifesto:* "Humanists regard the universe as self-existing and not created."[10] In short, atheists believe that the universe had no Creator or Cause: It is just there. Everything is nature. There is no supernatural.

   But even atheists are not usually content to let their atheism rest in "nonbelief." The universe perhaps isn't personal enough for their worship. Instead, they worship man! Paul Kurtz, in the same context quoted above, acknowledges the "religion of humanism": "To establish such a religion [of humanism] is a major necessity of the present."[11] In other parts of the same *Humanist Manifesto* we find:

> No deity will save us; we must save ourselves.[12]
> Religious humanism maintains that all associations and institutions exist for the fulfillment of human life.[13]

   This "deification" of man is nothing new. German philosopher and atheist Ludwig Feuerbach (1804-1872) boldly pronounced, "The divine being is nothing else than the human being."[14] Karl Marx (1818-1883), the "father" of communism, declared, "The criticism of religion ends with the teaching that man is the highest essence for man."[15]

   Religious atheism is popular today among a variety of atheists, and is incorporated into such atheistic religions as Marxism, Hina Yana Buddhism, and secular humanism. Contemporary psychologist and author Eric Fromm said, "God is not a symbol of power over man but of man's own powers."[16] Ayn Rand, cited above for her belief that matter is eternal, put it very clearly by saying, "I raise this god over the earth, this god whom men have sought since men came into being, this god who will grant them joy and peace and pride. This god, this one word: I."[17] One of Rand's disciples, Dr. Harry Binswanger, who is editor of the atheist magazine she founded, *The Objectivist,* stated in a public debate with me, "If you follow my philosophy you will create yourself in the image of an ideal, and then you should worship yourself." It is not correct to say that atheists have no belief: When an atheist worships his "God," he really worships himself!

When we discussed theism, we noted that our morality—our ethics, our sense of right and wrong—should derive from our dependence on God as our Creator and Sustainer. Since atheists do not believe in a Creator, but worship the universe or man, they cannot have a morality based on something outside the universe. Sigmund Freud (1856-1939), the "father" of psychoanalytic theory, attributed to illusion any morality based on God:

> It would be very nice if there were a God who created the world and was a benevolent Providence, and if there were a moral order in the universe and an after-life; but it is a very striking fact that all this is exactly as we are bound to wish it to be.[18]

God is viewed with disdain as a cosmic comforter or a heavenly Linus blanket—an immature and unrealistic retreat for those who can't handle reality.

What then shall we do if there is no God? Many atheists agree with atheistic philosopher Friedrich Nietzsche (1844-1900) that when God "died," all absolute values died with him. Since God does not exist, man must devise his own way of life. The late Jean-Paul Sartre, French atheist and playwright, added, "If God does not exist, [we are not] provided with any values or commands that could legitimate our behavior.... We are left alone, without excuse."[19] There can be no ethic based on something outside the universe, if there is nothing outside the universe!

This does not mean that there is no right or wrong for an atheist. It does mean, however, that God does not determine what is right and what is wrong: Man decides. In other words, values are not discovered by man and established by God; they have no need to be discovered because they are established by man. In short, when man dethrones God, he usually enthrones himself as God. The atheist is not without his gods, whether they are nature, mankind, or one's own ego. But the gods of atheism are not the only other "god options" available today. Let us now turn to the second of our six alternatives to Christian theism: the God of pantheism.

Pantheism

Pantheism is the belief that God is the universe. For a pantheist, as with an atheist, there is no Creator beyond the universe. However, for a pantheist there is a god, but he is identified with the universe. Creator and creation are two different ways of viewing one reality. God is the universe and the universe is God. There is ultimately only one reality, not many different ones. Many religions are identified with pantheism, including many forms of Hinduism,* Zen Buddhism,† and Christian Science (along with other modern-day mind-science cults). In addition, many people believe in pantheism without identifying themselves with a particular established religious belief. Pantheism is one of the fundamental beliefs of the New Age movement groups, and it underlies the world view of the ever-popular Star Wars saga. For pantheists, there is no absolute distinction between God and the universe or man. In fact, man is divine because he is part of God.

The Star Wars movies have attracted millions of moviegoers with their exciting stories of war, love, and the rescue of the cosmos. And at the center of Star Wars is the Force: "May the Force be with you"; "Prepare to meet the Force"; "My ally is the Force"; "Open yourself to the Force"; "Feel the

---

* Hinduism is the European name for the religion of India, which developed over a long period of time as an effort to harmonize or unify all of the multiplicity of beliefs (pantheistic, polytheistic, and even monotheistic) which were held by the thousands of different localized religious bodies.

† Zen Buddhism is a Japanese meditation form of Buddhism.

Force.'' These phrases leap from the Star Wars screen. What is the Force?

According to series creator George Lucas, "It is an energy field generated by living things."[20] Having identified the Force with the energy of life, Lucas notes its all-encompassing nature: "It envelopes you as it radiates from you."[21] The Force has two sides, a good (light) side and a bad (dark) side. This is very like the dualism prevalent in many forms of religious pantheism, including some forms of Hinduism. Lucas' Force can be used to predict the future as well as to perform super-normal events such as levitation.

Lucas identifies the Force with God: "There is a God and there is both a good side and a bad side. You have a choice between them, but the world works better if you're on the good side."[22]

The producer of the second Star Wars film, Irvin Kershner, appeals to Zen Buddhism as an ingredient in the Star Wars philosophy, and identifies the Force with the TAO (the "way," "path," or "eternal principle") of Zen Buddhism: "I wanna introduce some Zen here because I don't want the kids to walk away just feeling that everything is shoot-'em-up, but that there's also a little something to think about there in terms of yourself and your surroundings."[23]

A very popular contemporary religious philosophy has been dubbed the "New Age movement," which is a loosely knit movement of religious and quasireligious groups which hold certain beliefs in common. The New Age movement groups hold to pantheism, mysticism, some commitment to global unity as an expression of the "oneness" of everything, and "cosmic humanism," a belief which sees man as the measure of all things (humanism) because of his identity with the divine cosmos. One New Age movement writer, Benjamin Creme, described God this way: "God is the sum total of all that exists in the whole of the manifested and unmanifested universe."[24]

Oscar-winning actress Shirley MacLaine, a committed rein-carnationist, declared in her bestselling autobiography *Out on a Limb*: "The tragedy of the human race was that we had forgotten we were all Divine."[25]

This is pantheism, whether elaborately ritualistic and religious (as in some forms of Hinduism) or subtly assumed and lived out (as in Star Wars). Pantheism has confused the creation with the Creator, assuming one to be the other. I consider atheism and pantheism the two greatest threats to Christianity in the contemporary Western "belief marketplace." In later chapters we will see how pantheism is attacking God, Christ, and miracles.

Let us turn now to a brief survey of the other belief options we included in our chart.

Panentheism

Panentheism says that God is in the universe like a mind is in a body. The universe is God's "body." God's "body" and his "mind" (or soul) are seen as two "poles." The physical universe, his body, is his "actual pole." His mind, his immaterial part, is eternal and infinite and is called his "potential pole."

There are very few religious groups, and no major world religions, which hold a panentheistic view of God. Westerners who have been exposed to panentheism have probably encountered it in the writings of some liberal Western theologians (sometimes called "process theologians") as a sort of philosophical panentheism. The four leading panentheistic theologians in the West include Alfred Whitehead, Charles Hartshorne, Shubert Ogden, and John Cobb.

Both pantheism (discussed above) and panentheism hold some things in common. Both deny any absolute or essential distinction between God and the world. Both believe that the universe is eternal. Both believe that the universe is made of the essence of God (although the two views differ in explaining that relationship).

But pantheism and panentheism also differ from each other in some important respects. Some of these differences are listed below.

PANTHEISM	PANENTHEISM
God is the universe	God is in the universe
God is personal	God is not personal
God is infinite	God is finite
God is eternal	God is temporal
God is unchanging	God is changing
God and creatures are identical	God and creatures are not identical

The panentheistic God/universe setup is like a mutual admiration society: God needs you, and you need God. Alfred Whitehead said, "Apart from God, there would be no actual world; and apart from the actual world with its creativity, there would be no rational explanation of the ideal vision which constitutes God."[26] God depends on the world, and the world depends on God.

The panentheistic God does not create the world out of nothing, as the Christian God does, but forms it out of his own "primordial nature." The panentheistic God "is not before all creation, but with all creation."[27]

Panentheists say that God has two "poles": His "actualized" pole is the universe, and his "potential" pole is beyond the physical universe. He has a potential nature and an actual nature. His potential nature is God's ideal vision, and his actual nature is what he has actually attained at any given moment.

Since God is always growing, or "in process," he never perfectly achieves his aims. In metaphorical terms, God is always on the path but he never reaches his destination. The actual is what he is; the potential is what he is eternally becoming. Panentheist Charles Hartshorne described how we are co-creators with and of God:

God in his concrete de facto state is in one sense

simply self-made, like every creature spontaneously springing into being as something more than any causal antecedents could definitely imply. In another sense, or causally speaking, God, in his latest concrete state, is jointly "made" or produced by God and the world in the prior states of each. We are not simply co-creators, with God, of the world, but in last analysis, co-creators with him, of himself.[28]

This panentheistic God has other limitations. The panentheistic God is not omnipotent: He operates the world through persuasion only. Evil is that which is resistant to God's persuasion. Since God is not omnipotent, the best he can do is to be generally victorious over evil. He can never completely vanquish evil.

This leads to a novel, though wrong, approach to answering the atheist's challenge concerning evil: If God is all-powerful and all-good, why is there evil in the world? The panentheist can answer: He isn't all-powerful. He can't get rid of evil.

The limited God of panentheism is only one of the views of God which pictures God as limited. We will now turn to a brief look at finite godism.

Finite Godism

Finite godism states that a finite God exists beyond and in the universe. Finite godism is somewhat like theism, except that its God is not infinite but limited in his nature and power. Unlike the sophisticated bipolar God of panentheism, the finite God is simply one in his limited nature. This is not a systematized religious view, but has been held by various individuals at times over the last 2000 years. The ancient Greek philosopher Plato, as well as later philosophers such as John Stuart Mill, William James, and more recently Edgar Sheffield Brightman and Peter Bertocci, affirmed finite godism.

Finite godism has enjoyed a sort of vogue since the Second World War as a response to the horrors of the holocaust: Maybe God *couldn't* have prevented the atrocities of the war. Many people today in America have heard of (or have read) the bestselling book *When Bad Things Happen to Good People*, by Rabbi Kushner. He declares, "God wants the righteous to live peaceful, happy lives, but sometimes He can't bring that about...there are some things God does not control."[29]

Finite godists have wrestled with the problem of suffering in this world, and think that their view is the only reasonable answer. Philosopher John Stuart Mill stated:

> Nature impales men, breaks them as if on the wheel, casts them to be devoured by wild beasts, burns them to death, crushes them with stones like the first Christian martyr, starves them with hunger, freezes them with cold, poisons them by the quick or slow venom of her exhalations, and has hundreds of other hideous deaths in reserve, such as the ingenious cruelty of a Nabis or a Domitian never surpassed. All this, Nature does with the most supercilious disregard both of mercy and of justice, emptying her shafts upon the best and noblest indifferently with the meanest and worst.[30]

Philosopher and professor (at Boston University) Peter Bertocci recites the logic of the finite godist this way:

> If God is omnipotent, and therefore the creator of so much evil, how can He be good? Or if He is good, and did not intend evil, can He be omnipotent in the sense defined? Must there not be something beyond the control of His good will which is the source of evil in the world?[31]

In short, a finite godist believes that God is the designer of the universe but is not the all-powerful and/or all-perfect designer.

Deism

Deism is like theism without miracles. God exists *beyond* the world but not *in* it in any supernatural way. Deism insists that there must have been a creator or originator of the universe, but that this creator does not interfere in the universe. There are no supernatural events—only natural events.

While many people assume that the founding fathers of the United States of America were Christians, the truth is that deism was more influential than Christian theism in shaping our country. Thomas Jefferson, author of the Declaration of Independence, believed in "nature's God," who "created all men equal" and endowed them with "inalienable rights" in accordance with the "laws of nature."

Thomas Jefferson rejected all miracles. He declared, "The day will come when the account of the birth of Christ as accepted in the Trinitarian churches will be classed with the fable of Minerva springing from the brain of Jupiter."[32] Jefferson literally cut all of the miracles from the four Gospels. He said:

> There will be found remaining the most sublime and benevolent code of morals which has ever been offered to man. I have performed this operation for my own use, by cutting verse by verse out of the printed book, and arranging the matter which is evidently his and which is as easily distinguished as diamonds in a dunghill.[33]

Deists reject the Bible as the supernatural revelation of God. Another founding father of America, Thomas Paine, viciously attacked both the Bible and Christianity, saying of Christianity:

> Of all the systems of religion that ever were invented, there is none more derogatory to the Almighty, more unedifying to man, more repugnant to reason, and more contradictory in itself, than this thing called Christianity. Too absurd for belief, too

impossible to convince, and too inconsistent for
practice, it renders the heart torpid, or produces only
atheists and fanatics. As an engine of power, it serves
the purpose of despotism; and as a means of wealth,
the avarice of priests; but so far as respects the good
of man in general, it leads to nothing here or here-
after.[34]

Deists believe in the moral laws of God, and prayer, and
even the providence of God. At the end of George Washing-
ton's administration a treaty was signed which denied that we
were a "Christian" nation. The treaty read, in part, "As the
Government of the United States of America is not in any sense
founded on the Christian Religion...."[35] This accommodated
deistic belief.

Deists reject any supernatural intervention by God into the
natural world once he had made it. God is to the world what
a master mechanic is to his machine. Like the atheist, the deist
bars all supernatural events from the world. The deistic God
is directly opposed to the supernatural God of the Bible.

Polytheism

Polytheism says that there are many finite gods in the
universe who influence the world. Polytheists deny an infinite
God beyond the world, which is a theistic view. There are many
examples of polytheistic religions and religious groups throughout history and around the world. The gods of ancient Greece,
ancient Rome, and modern-day Mormonism are examples of
polytheistic gods.

Like the finite gods, the gods of polytheism are limited in
their power. Usually they operate in limited domains of the
natural world and are especially associated with particular
natural phenomena, such as the god of rain or the god of wind.

Polytheism is not just a primitive pagan belief that ancient
cultures held. It is enjoying a widespread revival today, even
in America. This growing phenomenon was noted by David

L. Miller, Associate Professor of Religion at New York's Syracuse University, in his 1974 book *The New Polytheism: Rebirth of the Gods and Goddesses*. He argues that, since God has "died" in Western society, there is no longer "a single center holding things together.... The death of God has given rise to the birth of the gods."[36]

The lure of polytheism to Westerners is explained by Miller, who says that the polytheist is "relieved from a puritan sense of duty to perfection and completeness.... He will experiment, first with this God and then that Goddess. He will return to the Gods who have been forgotten and repressed."[37]

While there are many forms of polytheism enjoying greater or lesser popularity in America today, Miller thinks that ancient Greek polytheism is the most prevalent: "Greece is the locus of polytheism simply because, willy-nilly, we are occidental men and women."[38]

The largest and fastest-growing polytheistic religion in America today, Mormonism, has generated its own gods and goddesses. Mormonism is the common name given to the Church of Jesus Christ of Latter-day Saints, founded on April 6, 1830, by Joseph Smith, Jr., a former buried-treasure-seeker. Smith claimed that God the Father and Jesus Christ (two separate gods) had called him to "restore" true Christianity to the earth. Walter Martin, Christian theologian and expert on the cults and the occult, noted the clear distinction between Mormon theology and Christian theology:

> If one sentence could be used to sum up the difference between Mormonism and Christianity, it could be said without fear of contradiction that Mormonism is polytheistic and Christianity is monotheistic.... The Mormon Church defines the doctrine of the Trinity as actually a belief in three separate gods, which is not monotheism but tritheism.[39]

Consistently throughout the history of the Mormon church,

polytheism (the belief in multiplicity of gods) has been affirmed. (This affirmation is much more clear within the church than it is in the professional advertising for the Mormon religion, which attempts to make Mormonism look like just another denomination of Christianity.)

Mormon founder Joseph Smith, Jr., taught that the God of this earth was an exalted man who had developed into godhood, just as had all gods before him and just as faithful Mormons would in the future:

> God himself was once as we are now, and is an exalted man, and sits enthroned in yonder heavens!... I am going to tell you how God came to be God. We have imagined and supposed that God was God from all eternity. I will refute that idea.... Here, then, is eternal life—to know the only wise and true God; and you have got to learn how to be gods yourselves...the same as all gods have done before you.[40]

> The heads of the Gods appointed one god for us; and when you take view of the subject, it sets one free to see all the beauty, holiness and perfection of the Gods.... Many men say there is one God; the Father, the Son and the Holy Ghost are only one God! I say that is a strange God anyhow—three in one, and one in three! It is a curious organization.... All are to be crammed into one God, according to sectarianism. It would make the biggest God in all the world. He would be a wonderfully big God—he would be a giant or a monster.[41]

Brigham Young was the second leader of the Mormons (after the death of Joseph Smith). He is the leader who orchestrated the Mormon migration to Utah and who established and ruled Salt Lake City and the surrounding regions. He also taught the plurality of gods:

> How many Gods there are, I do not know. But

there never was a time when there were no Gods and worlds. . . . [42]

The many gods of the various forms of polytheism marketed in America today all vie for the allegiance of men and women. None of these systems or gods are true. There is only one true God, the God of the Bible, who said, "You shall have no other gods before me" (Exodus 20:3 NIV). Polytheism is false.

Conclusion

In our survey of belief systems, we have seen that there are several possible categories of belief about God. Either there is no god(s) (atheism) or there is. If there is, then there are either many gods (polytheism) or there is only one god. If there is only one god, then he either is actually identified with the universe (pantheism and panentheism) or he is not. If he is not, then either he is finite (finite godism) or infinite. If infinite, then either he performs no miracles (deism) or he does perform miracles (theism). Theism is the kind of belief in God that the Bible teaches and that Christians believe. While we have surveyed all of the logically possible types, we have concentrated on the beliefs of atheism and pantheism, the largest threats to Christian theism in America today. Let us now turn to how atheism and pantheism are threatening Christianity. We will look first at atheism's attack on the Christian God.

CHAPTER 3

Atheism Attacks God

The true God, the theistic God of the Bible, the Creator and Sustainer of all things, has come under severe attack from two major fronts today: atheism and pantheism. Atheists claim that there is nothing in existence but the universe. Pantheists insist that God is the universe. Both attack Christian theism. By humorous analogy, we could say that both want to devour the Christian God. The atheists want to chew Him up (reduce him to nothing) and spit him out (say that he does not exist), while the pantheists want to chew him up (reduce him to the creation) and swallow him (make him one with the universe). Strict materialism* and pantheistic mysticism have the same purpose: denying the Christian God. In this chapter we will consider the atheistic attack on the Christian God.

Atheism's Broadsword

First we will consider some of the general attacks on Christian theism given by atheists. For all practical purposes,

---

* Materialism is the point of view that only the material universe is real.

atheism and agnosticism are the same. The word "atheism" comes from the Greek *a* (without) and *theos* (God). An atheist believes that no god(s) exist. Agnosticism comes from the Greek *a* (without) and *gnosis* (knowledge). An agnostic does not know if God exists. He may not have enough knowledge himself right now, but he believes that such knowledge is at least hypothetically obtainable. Or he may believe that such knowledge is forever out of the reach of any human. Atheists struggle with the problem of the existence of God, while agnostics struggle with the problem of knowledge.

However, both live their lives and argue as though no God exists. The late Bertrand Russell, popular advocate against theism, admitted that "an Agnostic may think the Christian God as improbable as the Olympians; in that case, he is, for practical purposes, at one with the atheists."[1] Atheists sometimes criticize agnostics, as when Karl Marx said, "What, indeed, is agnosticism but...'shamefaced' materialism? The agnostic's conception of nature is materialistic throughout."[2] But despite the differences, both agnostics and atheists unite against theism in insisting that God plays no role in their understanding of the world. Both have the same materialistic world view. Both join in insisting that there are no rational grounds for believing in the existence of God. For the purposes of this book, we will treat agnosticism and atheism as one world view.

Make no mistake about it: Atheism attacks Christian theism. The atheism popular in America today is aggressive in its denial of God, and follows a long tradition of atheistic attack on God. Gary DeYoung, vice president of the atheistic Free Thought Society of America, says:

> Buddy, you ain't seen nothing yet! This is more than an emergency for you superstitious neanderthals [Christians]. You are absolutely correct, we fully intend to destroy superstition in the United States of America for once and for all.
> We threw superstition out of the schools, next we will throw the chaplains off the battleships, and we

will teach American children that Tyrannosaurus was
not on Noah's ark.[3]

George Smith, author of a popular contemporary atheist
book, states:

> It is my purpose, however, to demonstrate that
> the belief in god is irrational to the point of absur-
> dity; and that this irrationality, when manifested in
> specific religions such as Christianity, is extremely
> harmful.[4]

Contemporary atheists are copying their predecessors, who
also attacked Christian theism. The famous German atheist,
Friedrich Nietzsche, experienced the Christian God "as
miserable, as absurd, as harmful, not merely as an error but
as a crime against life...we deny God as God."[5] Philosopher
Thomas J. J. Altizer decided that modern man had outgrown
any need for God, and so he popularized a "death of God"
theology: "In this world, as we have seen, there is no need
for religion and no need for God.... This refusal is made
inevitable by the scientific revolution of the seventeenth
century...."[6]

The late Ayn Rand, quoted earlier in this book, said, "That
dark, incoherent passion within you, which you take as the
voice of God or of your glands, is nothing more than the corpse
of your mind."[7] Carl Sagan, popular astronomer and host of
the award-winning Cosmos television series, stated, "It is said
that men may not be the dreams of the gods, but rather that
the gods are the dreams of men."[8] These are only a few of
the loud voices raised against the existence of God.

The "Aims and Purposes" of the American Atheists organization, founded by well-known atheist Madalyn Murray
O'Hair, include "to develop and propagate a social philosophy
in which man is the central figure who alone must be the source
of strength, progress and ideals for the well-being and happi-
ness of humanity." This statement also defines atheism and
materialism as follows:

> Atheism is the life philosophy *(Weltanschauung)*
> of persons who are free from theism. It is predicated
> on the ancient Greek philosophy of Materialism....
> The Materialist philosophy declares that the cosmos
> is devoid of imminent conscious purpose; that it is
> governed by its own inherent, immutable and
> impersonal law; that there is no supernatural inter-
> ference in human life; that man—finding his
> resources with himself—can and must create his own
> destiny; and that his potential for good and higher
> development is for all practical purposes unlimited.[9]

That atheists are attacking the Christian God has been established. How they are attacking the Christian God is the subject
of the rest of this chapter. I will start first with a summary
of particular arguments for the existence of God which atheists
attack. Then I will examine the way atheists commonly counter
and/or criticize each of those arguments.

God As the Uncaused Cause

One argument often advanced for the existence of God is,
stated briefly, "Every effect has a cause. The universe is an
effect. It must have a cause. God, who is not an effect himself, is that cause. God is the uncaused cause."

The atheistic argument against God goes like this:

1. Theists conceive of God as a self-caused being.
2. But a self-caused being is irrational.
3. Therefore, the very concept of God is irrational.

But this atheist objection is based on a "straw man" argument in that it attempts to refute what theists don't even
believe. The theist does not claim that God is *self-caused*, but
rather that he is *uncaused*. A self-caused being is impossible,
but an uncaused being is not.

Zeroing in on a particular aspect of that argument, the atheist
can also claim that it is irrational to say that God is uncaused.

They insist that it is reasonable to ask, "Who made God?"

The atheist organization called The Free Thought Association publishes a booklet by atheist spokesman Gordon Stein entitled *How to Argue with a Theist (and Win)*. Stein raises this criticism:

> If everything must have had a cause, then God must have had a cause. If God had a cause, then He was not the first (or uncaused) cause. If God did not have a cause, then not everything must have a cause. If not everything needs a cause, then perhaps the universe is one of those things which also does not need a cause.[10]

As this shows, some atheists contend that theists are irrational because they believe that since God has no cause beyond himself, therefore he must be the cause of his own existence. The reason for this is that a cause must be prior to its effect (if not in time, at least in being). But it is impossible to be prior to oneself. One cannot exist before he exists. He cannot lift himself up by his own metaphysical bootstraps. However, put in this way, the atheists' argument is simply a "straw man," a false argument raised and then refuted. Theists do not agree with the first premise: "Theists conceive of God as a self-caused being," or "If everything must have had a cause, then God must have had a cause."

Theists first do not believe that God is self-caused; they believe he is uncaused. Second, theists do not believe that *everything* must have a cause, but only that every *effect* must have a cause. Atheists say, "Everything has a cause." Theists say, "Everything that *begins* has a cause." No theist believes that God created himself; we believe that God is the uncreated Creator.

If it is irrational to believe that God, who has no beginning, needs no cause, then atheism is irrational. Many atheists believe that the universe needs no cause because it had no beginning. The real question is, What is eternal? God, the cause of the universe? Or the universe itself? Agnostic Bertrand Russell said, "I should say that the Universe is just there, and that's all." As Carl Sagan put it, "If we say that God has always existed, why not save a step and conclude that the universe has always existed?"[11]

If the atheist believes that it is rational to claim that the universe could simply be there forever without a cause, then there is no reason why God could not have been there forever without a cause.

The whole question boils down to whether the universe is eternal or had a beginning. If it had a beginning, then it is rational to believe that it had a Creator. If the universe is eternal, then it is rational to believe that it had no Creator.

Even some agnostic scientists now are admitting that there is strong scientific evidence that the universe had a beginning. The agnostic astrophysicist Dr. Robert Jastrow, who is founder and director of the Goddard Institute for Space Research, said, "Science has proven that the universe exploded into being at a certain moment...the scientist's pursuit of the past ends in the moment of creation."[12]

Dr. Jastrow points to several areas of scientific evidence to support his conclusion: "Now three lines of evidence—the motions of the galaxies, the laws of thermodynamics, and the life story of the stars—pointed to one conclusion: all indicated that the universe had a beginning."[13]

The extreme to which atheists are willing to go in avoiding the evidence and its rational conclusion that there was a Creator of the universe is typified by the British philosopher Anthony Kenny:

> According to the Big Bang theory, the whole matter of the universe began to exist at a particular time in the remote past. A proponent of such a theory, at least if he is an atheist, must believe that the matter of the universe came from nothing and by nothing.[14]

There it is—the ultimate absurdity. The atheist says nothing made something! By contrast, the theist says Someone (God) made something. In view of this, it is strange indeed that we hear atheism calling theism irrational! It is not the theist who misconceives God, but the atheist who misconceives the theist's God. Theism is rational and atheism's charge is irrelevant.

Arguing from the Parts to the Whole

Another theistic argument uses the individual things we can observe to surmise about the entire universe: "Every single thing we observe in this universe is dependent on something else, or caused. If every part of the universe is caused, then the sum of those parts, the universe itself, must be caused. The cause of the universe we identify with God."

Atheists often argue that theism is irrational because it assumes that the whole must have the same characteristics as the parts. This is called the fallacy of composition in logic. It is illustrated by the following diagram:

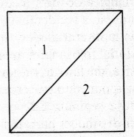

The theist will point out that, simply because each part of the overall figure is a triangle, that does not mean that the figure as a whole is a triangle. Indeed, it is not a triangle. It is a square. Likewise, the atheist sees the same fallacy in this kind of reasoning by a theist. However, let's look more carefully at the atheists' example and at the argument itself.

When the Whole Is Like Its Parts

Consider the following illustration. Suppose there is a floor in which each tile is green. Would it not also be true that the whole floor is also green? If every part of a pair of scissors were metal, then the whole scissors would be metal too. In the same way, if every part of the universe is dependent or caused, then the whole universe is caused.

To understand why the atheists' counter example does not apply to the universe, and why the floor or scissors example does, requires a little bit of knowledge about terms. Two important terms I will use here are accidental and essential. *Accidental* is "that quality which adheres to a subject in such a manner that it neither constitutes its essence nor necessarily flows from its essence."[15] In other words, it is an attribute of something that is not necessary to that thing. For example, whether a man has blue eyes or brown eyes is accidental to being human. Eye color is accidental. *Essential* is "definition of the elements of a thing."[16] In other words, as we defined it before, a thing's essence is what makes it what it is, and not something else. Now, with these two definitions, let's look at our argument again.

Of course two triangles do not necessarily add up to a triangle. This is because it is accidental to triangles that when they are combined with other triangles, they sometimes make squares. But it is essential to triangles to be geometric figures, and that, when they are added together, they will make a larger geometric form, not a nongeometric form.

In the same way, it is essential to a dependent part that, when it is added to another dependent part, the two are still dependent parts. We never get something independent simply by adding up dependent parts. They must all be dependent on something which ultimately is independent.

An atheist may object to this reasoning, insisting that it implies that the sum is always equal to its parts and then contending that the whole may be more than its parts. For example, a whole car is more than all its parts scattered over a parking lot. The parts in the lot lack unity or wholeness. So, argues the atheist, the universe as a whole may be uncaused, even though all its parts are caused.

An Independent Universe?

Let us probe the atheists' argument from a different angle. Does this "unity" of the dependent parts of the universe actually make the universe as a whole independent? What if every dependent part of the universe were destroyed? If all the dependent parts were destroyed, would we be left only with this "independent unity," this transcedent universe? No, this "uncaused whole" would go out of existence because it actually has no existence outside of its dependent parts; it must be dependent on its parts. It is actually not independent at all, but dependent. It is caused to exist by its parts. Now the atheists' argument is shown to be insufficient and inadequate.

The only rational way out of the dilemma for the atheist is to say that the whole is not dependent on the parts, and that it would not go out of existence even if its parts did. But what is the difference between what we call the Creator or first cause and the atheists' eternal, necessary, uncaused "whole beyond the parts" of the universe, which is the cause of everything that exists in the universe?

The atheist has only one of two ways to answer:

1. If the "whole" universe is caused, then there must be a cause outside of the universe itself.

2. If the whole universe is an independent, uncaused cause of everything that exists in the universe, then it possesses the same basic characteristics that the atheist is not willing to allow for the Creator.

Both ways lead to a theistic conclusion—namely, that a Creator or cause of the entire universe exists. So, while the atheists' argument sounds good at first, it actually turns out to be an argument for theism.

Who Made God?

Theists claim that God had no creator. He is eternal. One cannot go "back before" God, since there never was a time when God was not. On the contrary, God is the creator of everything else in existence.

However, atheists sometimes charge that there doesn't need to be a "first cause." Limited causes can go on forever. Even if the universe needs a cause, there is no reason why there needs to be a first cause. It is rational, they say, to assume an infinite series of limited causes.

As an analogy, atheists point out that infinite sets are an accepted part of mathematics. For example, there are an infinite number of points (which have no dimension) between A and B on any given line. Thus, they insist, it is also rational to assume that there could be an actual infinite number of causes stretching back into the infinite past. The atheists' argument can be summarized this way:

1. Infinite sets are rationally possible.

2. An infinite series of actual causes would be an actual infinite set.

3. Therefore, an infinite series of actual causes is rationally possible.

This argument says that maybe God made the universe, but who made God? And who made that God? And so on, forever.

Time and Infinity

Let's look at this closely. There are three fatal flaws in this argument. First, the conclusion (number 3) is already assumed in the second statement (number 2). Second, the atheist must assume that the universe is infinite. I do not accept that the universe or anything within it is infinite, and I have discussed some of my reasons for rejecting an infinite universe. Third, what is rationally possible does not necessarily have any correspondence to anything in the actual world. (Unicorns are rationally possible, but actually nonexistent.)

Christian philosopher Richard Purtill presents a clear and logical refutation to the atheists' contention:

> It seems to be logically possible for A to be caused by B, for B to be caused by C, and so on, backward ad infinitum. There is, however, a very serious objection to this sort of "infinite regress," as it is called....

For example, if A tries to borrow a lawnmower from B, and B replies, "I don't have one, but I'll borrow one from my friend C," and C says, "I don't have one but, I'll borrow one from my friend D," and so on, this is a case of the kind we are concerned with. Or if A asks B, his supervisor, for permission to take the afternoon off and B says, "I can't give you permission without asking my supervisor, C," and C says, "I can't give you permission to give A permission unless I ask my supervisor, D," and so on, we have a case of this sort.

Now in these ordinary cases two things are clear:

1. If the series of things that don't have the property in question goes on to infinity, the first individual never gets that property. If everyone asked says, "I don't have a lawnmower, but I'll ask," A never gets his lawnmower. If every supervisor asked says, "I can't give you permission, but I'll ask," then A never gets his afternoon off.

2. If the first thing *does* get the property in question, then the series comes to an end, and does not go on to infinity. If A gets his lawnmower, someone along the line had a lawnmower without having to borrow one. If A gets his afternoon off, some supervisor could give permission without having to ask someone else.[17]

Let's give another example to go with the lawnmower and the afternoon off. Think of an infinite number of actual moments extending back in time with no beginning. What do we have? We have an actual impossibility for the following reasons.

1. If there were an infinite number of moments before today, then today would never have arrived (because an infinite number of moments can never be completed).

2. But today has arrived.

3. Therefore, there were not an infinite number of moments before today.

This means that there were only a limited number of

moments before the present moment. In other words, the universe had a beginning. Even the great skeptic David Hume (1711-1776), whose arguments against miracles are still used today by atheists, saw the truth of the two reasons necessary to prove that the universe had a first cause. The argument can be stated this way:

1. Everything that begins has a cause.
2. The universe had a beginning.
3. Therefore the universe had a cause (Creator).

David Hume insisted that it would be absurd to deny the first statement:

> But allow me to tell you that I never asserted so absurd a proposition as that anything might arise without a cause: I only maintain'd, that our certainty of the falsehood of that proposition proceeded neither from intuition nor demonstration; but from another source.[18]

Hume affirmed the truth of the second statement in these words:

> An infinite number of real parts of time, passing in succession and exhausted one after another, appears so evident a contradiction that no man, one should think, whose judgment is not corrupted, instead of being improved, by the sciences, would ever be able to admit it.[19]

Simple logic tells us that if these first two statements are true, then the third statement must be true. The universe must have had a cause. At least it is rational to affirm that it did, and irrational to deny it. Belief in a Creator of the universe is rational and disbelief is irrational.

Why Is the Cause God?

Theists go further than the above in stating that the universe not only had a cause, but that the cause of the universe is an intelligent, personal Creator. In simple form, here is a theistic argument for an intelligent Creator:

   1. The first living thing had highly complex information in it.

   2. Highly complex information regularly comes from an intelligent cause.

   3. Therefore, there was an intelligent cause of the first living thing.

However, some atheists insist that complex information could have evolved by mere chance (given enough time). They claim that it is not necessary to attribute the complex universe to an intelligent being.

Mathematical Odds

Even the atheist will admit, however, that the mathematical odds for even a single-celled animal to develop from pure chemicals (without intelligent direction) is infinitesimally small. Nobel-prize-winning scientist George Walk went so far as to say that it was even statistically impossible: "One has only to contemplate the magnitude of this task to concede that the spontaneous generation of a living organism is impossible."[20]

The thoroughgoing materialist, confronted with such a near-certain impossibility, will say, "But since we do have life today, it must have happened, no matter how remote the possibility." Here the materialist is betraying his anti-God bias. He is saying, "I don't accept that it could have happened your way, so it must have happened my way." It's like the story of the commuter and the elephants. Harry commuted by train between New York City and Connecticut every day. One day a man sat next to him, opened the window, and began throwing rubber bands out the window, one at a time, during the entire trip. The next day the man did the same thing. Every day Harry would watch the man throw rubber bands out the window. Finally Harry couldn't stand it any longer. "Excuse me," he said, "but why do you throw rubber bands out the window every day?" The man answered, "To scare the elephants away!'' ''But,'' Harry responded, ''there are no elephants in Connecticut!'' ''Precisely,'' replied the man. ''See how well it works?'' Enamored of his own pet theory, the man was unable to see what reason and a little bit of knowledge should have told him plainly.

Science, Reason, and Causes

But there is an even more fundamental objection to the atheists' faint hope in the possibility of a chance origin of life. Scientific reasoning is based not on chance happenings but on regular, causal connections.

Let's look at some illustrations. Even though it is mathematically possible that dropping a bomb in a printing factory will produce a Webster's Unabridged Dictionary, nevertheless it is not reasonable to believe that a dictionary would ever be caused in this manner. Likewise, even though it is remotely possible that a tornado raging through a junkyard could produce a Boeing 747, it is still reasonable to believe that all actual airplanes need an intelligent designer and builder. There may be some theoretical chance that wind and rain erosion could produce the faces of four presidents on the side of a mountain, but it is still far more reasonable to assume that an intelligent sculptor created Mount Rushmore.

Former atheist and eminent scientist Sir Fred Hoyle recently changed his mind about the need for an intelligent Creator of life when he looked objectively at the evidence:

> The trouble is that there are about two thousand enzymes, and the chance of obtaining them all in a random trial is only one part in $(10^{20}) = 10^{40000}$, an outrageously small probability that could not be faced even if the whole universe consisted of organic soup. . . . No matter how large the environment one considers, life cannot have had a random beginning. Troops of monkeys thundering away at random on typewriters could not produce the works of Shakespeare, for the practical reason that the whole

observable universe is not large enough to contain the necessary typewriters [and] the waste paper baskets required for the deposition of wrong attempts. The same is true for living material.[21]

Materialism by Faith

Of course, atheists do not have to accept what is reasonable. Even if one grants that there are various ways to calculate the odds, no matter which way you calculate them, the chance of life arising spontaneously is almost infinitely smaller than an even 50-50. Some atheists refuse to accept such a statistical argument, but have nothing better to offer by way of explanation. Instead, they hope that some as-yet-unknown future scientific discovery will clear up the mysteries in harmony with materialism. Russell F. Doolittle summarized his critique of such "probability creationism" as follows:

> Comfort yourself also with the fact that a mere thirty years ago...no one had the slightest inkling how proteins were genetically coded. Given the rapid rate of progress in our understanding of molecular biology, I have no doubt that satisfactory explanations of the problems posed here soon will be forthcoming.[22]

In other words, the atheist bases his view on a nebulous faith in something which may or may not be found in the future!

Why is it not reasonable to believe these things? Because scientific thinking is based on regularly observed causal connections. And we do not observe anything like this happening regularly. Nor can anyone do it by experimentation (without deliberate manipulation). Since science is based on regularly observed connections, not on long-shot odds or lucky shots, it is not scientific or reasonable to believe in a purely chance origin of first life.

Instead, it is reasonable to believe in an intelligent cause of life because life has complex information in it, and uniform experience shows that such information comes from intelligent beings. When we see even a few words written in the sky, such as "Tan Don't Burn," we assume that the words had an intelligent cause. This is because it is the basis for scientific analysis, using the principle of regularity. Simply put, whenever there is a singular event with an unknown cause, we assume that it had the same kind of cause as other events that occur regularly. We say this because scientific analysis is based on previous experience by which we know that only an intelligent cause can regularly produce complex information such as is found in a living cell.

Proving Life in Space

A contemporary scientific example concerns astronomy. Many scientists, including popular astronomer Carl Sagan, believe that even a single message from outer space would prove that there are intelligent beings there. Such scientists have even set up radio telescopes and recorders to listen for such signals. The project is known as Search for Extraterrestrial Intelligence (SETI). Sagan wrote, "The receipt of a single message from space would show that it is possible to live through such technological adolescence: the transmitting civilization, after all, has survived. Such knowledge, it seems to me, might be worth a great price."[23]

Just how can scientists be so sure from one simple message from outer space that it reflects an intelligent source? Couldn't it be merely an accidental or unusual combination of noises? Such a theory may be possible, but it is not reasonable. Regular experience tells us that even a simple intelligent message indicates an intelligent source. Even three letters in Morse Code—SOS—heard from a ship's radio during a raging storm would convince most people who heard it that an intelligent person in danger sent the message on purpose.

The Library of the Brain

If such simple bits of information as "Tan Don't Burn"

and "SOS" convince reasonable people of an intelligent source, then why don't the highly complex information packets found in living things convince scientists? The amount of complex information packed in living things is awesome, as noted by Carl Sagan:

> The information content of the human brain expressed in bits is probably comparable to the total number of connections among the neurons—about a hundred trillion, 10^{14}, bits. If written out in English, say, that information would fill some twenty million volumes, as many as in the world's largest libraries. The equivalent of twenty million books is inside the heads of every one of us. The brain is a very big place in a very small space.[24]

It stands to reason that if one assumes an intelligent cause for a single message from outer space, one should also assume an intelligent Creator for the 200 million volumes of information in the human brain! For anyone who might object that "information" is significantly different in a living cell from that in human language, it has been shown that the relationship between information in a living cell and that in a written language are mathematically identical.[25]

Recently three scientists wrote a book on *The Mystery of Life's Origin*. In it they argued for an intelligent Creator of first life as the only plausible conclusion in the light of all the evidence because—

> the undirected flow of energy through a primordial atmosphere and ocean is at present a woefully inadequate explanation for the incredible complexity associated with even simple living systems, and is probably wrong.[26]

How Do You Explain Evil?

Christian theists affirm that God is all-good and all-powerful, as well as all-knowing, but that his allowance for free will allows for the possibility of evil. The theist does not say that God causes evil or that he is unable to prevent evil, but that he allows evil as a consequence of free will. The Bible tells us that evil will not exist forever, and that a lifetime in the midst of evil and suffering is insignificant compared to eternity in perfect peace with God. The apostle Paul said it this way: "For I consider that the sufferings of this present time are not worthy to be compared with the glory that is to be revealed to us" (Romans 8:18).

However, a favorite contention of atheists is that the existence of evil in the world shows that the Christian God does not exist. One of the most forceful ways this argument is stated is like this:

1. If God is all-powerful, he could destroy evil.
2. If God is all-good, he would destroy evil.
3. But evil is not destroyed.
4. Therefore, no such God exists.

The great skeptic and philosopher David Hume (1711-1776) questioned the Christian God's existence on this basis: "Is he willing to prevent evil, but not able? Then is he impotent. Is he able, but not willing? Then is he malevolent. Is he both able and willing? Whence then is evil?"[27]

Other types of godists can offer options to the problem. A finite godist would say that God is not all-powerful or all-good. This is the conclusion that Rabbi Kushner came to in his best-selling book, *When Bad Things Happen to Good People*. He wrote, "God wants the righteous to live peaceful, happy lives, but sometimes even He can't bring that about. It is too difficult even for God to keep cruelty and chaos from claiming their innocent victims."[28]

What can the Christian theist answer to this atheistic attack? Is it rational to believe in an all-good and all-powerful God in the face of evil? In order to answer this, let us look more closely at the atheists' argument.

Evil and Free Will

First of all, the word "destroy" can be understood in two

ways. It can mean "annihilate completely," in its strongest sense, or else simply "to defeat entirely."

Moral evil is evil by choice. It is evil for which some agent is morally responsible. Moral good is goodness by choice. It is good for which some agent is morally responsible. It is impossible for God to destroy completely (annihilate) the possibility of all moral evil without also destroying (annihilating) its converse, the possibility of all moral good. Neither moral evil nor moral good can occur without free will.

Stones and animals cannot sin. They have no moral free choice. If God destroyed all free creatures, or at least their evil thoughts and actions, he would destroy free will, destroying any chance for moral evil or moral goodness. For when it becomes impossible to hate, then it also become impossible to love. And when it becomes impossible to blaspheme God, it also becomes impossible to worship him.

The Atheist and Free Will

Picture what would happen to the poor atheist if God took away free will. What, for example, would atheist Madalyn Murray O'Hair say if, when she opened her atheistic mouth to speak against God, he would fill it with cotton? Or, if every time she even started to think an atheistic thought, God would give her an Excedrin headache? Certainly she would protest (if only she could) that these were unjust invasions of her right to free thought and free speech!

So the only way for God to actually destroy the possibility (and actuality) of all evil would be for God to destroy all free choice. This argument can be summarized as follows:

1. The only way to destroy all evil is to destroy all free thought and choice.

2. Even atheists do not want their freedom of thought and choice destroyed.

3. Therefore, even atheists do not really want God to destroy all evil.

Evil and God's Patience

The second definition of "destroy," as mentioned above, is to defeat evil without destroying free creatures. If this is possible, and it involves no actual contradiction, then the atheists' argument cannot stand. Let us restate the atheists' argument in the light of this distinction. We will see that the last statement, the conclusion to the argument, does not follow logically from the previous statements:

1. An all-good God would defeat evil.
2. An all-powerful God could defeat evil.
3. But evil is not yet defeated.
4. Therefore, no such God exists.

Once we know that God has not yet defeated evil, the old conclusion does not follow. This is because it is possible that God may yet defeat evil at some time in the future. If so, then the conclusion doesn't follow. As a matter of fact, if God is all-good and all-powerful, then it is reasonable to believe that he *will* defeat evil in the future. This is because if God is all-good, he would want to do it, and if he is all-powerful, then he can do what he wants to do. Therefore, it is reasonable to expect that he will yet do it. This is exactly what the Bible teaches!

The All-Knowing Atheist

There is only one way that an atheist can salvage his argument at this point. This is how the salvaged argument would have to go:

1. An all-good God would defeat evil.
2. An all-powerful God could defeat evil.
3. But evil is not yet defeated and never will be defeated.
4. Therefore, there is no such God.

However, the atheist has a serious problem with the added phrase, "Evil will never be defeated." Just how does the atheist know this? Is he all-knowing? Can he see all future events with absolute certainty? If so, then the atheist would have to be

God. In short, the argument would have to assume the vantage point of God in order to be provable. Thus, in effect, the atheist would have to be God in order to disprove God. The atheist cannot provide a good reason to abandon belief in an all-good, all-powerful God.

C. S. Lewis, quoted in the previous chapter, stated well the circular nature of his own reasoning against God from evil before he became a Christian:

> My argument against God was that the universe seemed so cruel and unjust. But how had I got this idea of just and unjust? A man does not call a line crooked unless he has some idea of a straight line. What was I comparing this universe with when I called it unjust? Of course I could have given up my idea of justice by saying it was nothing but a private idea of my own. But if I did that, then my argument against God collapsed too.... Thus in the very act of trying to prove that God did not exist...I found I was forced to assume that one part of reality—namely my idea of justice—was full of sense.[29]

In short, again the atheist assumes God to disprove God.

Why People Really Reject God

This raises the question as to why people reject God. In the last analysis, atheism is primarily a matter of the heart, not of the head. As the apostle Paul put it in Romans 1:18-20:

> For the wrath of God is revealed from heaven against all ungodliness and unrighteousness of men, who suppress the truth in unrighteousness, because that which is known about God is evident within them; for God made it evident to them. For since the creation of the world His invisible attributes, His

eternal power and divine nature, have been clearly
seen, being understood through what has been made,
so that they are without excuse.

Notice that the Bible declares that all men—without
exception—"know about God." But what is "evident to them"
is nevertheless "repressed" by them (v. 18). So it is not a matter
of brain power but of willpower. Atheism is not so much theoretical as it is moral.

The German atheist Nietzsche said stubbornly, "We deny
God as God. If one were to prove this God of the Christians
to us, we should be even less able to believe in him."[30]

This is not a reason but a reaction. It is not a rational
response but an emotional outburst.

The real cause of atheism is not the lack of rational proof
for God, but the presence of rebellious pride against God. It
is the spectacle of the creature shaking his fist at the Creator
and declaring, "I refuse to believe in you even if you are there!"

Atheists, having forsaken the only Lord who could have res-
cued them from their own self-centeredness, are left with nothing but false pride. French atheist and existential philosopher
Jean-Paul Sartre (1905-1981) confessed to giving up belief in
God when he was convicted of wrongdoing:

> Only once did I have the feeling that He existed.
> I had been playing with matches and burned a small
> rug. I was in the process of covering up my crime
> when suddenly God saw me. I felt His gaze inside
> my head and on my hands.... I flew into a rage
> against so crude an indiscretion, I blasphemed....
> He never looked at me again.[31]

Sartre's story of rebellion against God doesn't end here. The
"Hound of Heaven" kept chasing him. Sartre had managed
to dismiss God the Father, but the Holy Spirit was relentless
in his pursuit. Sartre wrote, "I had all the more difficulty of
getting rid of Him in that He had installed Himself at the back

of my head...[but] I collared the Holy Ghost in the cellar and threw Him out; atheism is a cruel and long-range affair: I think I've carried it through.''[32]

But did Sartre "win" against God once and for all? Perhaps not. Shortly before Sartre's death he spent a great deal of time with an ex-Maoist and theist, Pierre Victor, who had a profound effect on the old philosopher's bitter atheism. In a dialogue between the two in the pages of the *Nouvel Observateur*, Sartre abandoned utterly his existential atheism, saying, "I do not feel that I am the product of chance, a speck of dust in the universe, but someone who was expected, prepared, prefigured. In short, a being whom only a Creator could put here: and this idea of a creating hand refers to God.''[33]

We conclude our review of atheism's attack on God by stating that atheism does not result from any lack of evidence that God is there, but rather from a willful reaction to the evidence that God is truly there.

CHAPTER 4

Pantheism Attacks God

Pantheism is as antagonistic to the Christian God as is atheism. Both pantheism and atheism are opposed to the eternal and infinite God who created the world out of nothing and who is absolutely distinct from it.

What Is Pantheism?

Pantheism comes from two Greek words: *panta,* meaning "all" or "everything," and *theos,* meaning "God." The pantheist believes that God is all or all is God. The pantheist identifies God with the universe, the nonmaterial world with the material world. The pantheist believes that all of existence, however superficially differentiated, is actually of one divine substance or essence.* Thus pantheism is completely contrary to biblical revelation, which makes a sharp, essential distinction

---

* The philosophical term *monism* is the idea that all of reality is of one substance, and has been proposed variously throughout the history of philosophy, beginning with the Greek philosopher Zeno of Elea.

between God, who is the Creator, and the universe, which is created (Isaiah 44:24).

Contemporary Pantheism

Pantheism is not compatible with monotheism. Many popular pantheistic ideas and religious groups in America today trace the origin of their philosophies to just a few sources. Two significant sources are Theosophy and/or a book by Levi (see below), or to recent importations of Eastern, usually Hindu, ideas brought here and popularized by Eastern "gurus." For example, guru Bhagwan Shree (Sir God) Rajneesh, whose pantheism underlies his unique Yoga philosophy, declared his defiance of Christianity this way:

> Not only is LSD a drug, Christianity is also, and a far more complex and subtle drug which gives you a sort of blindness. You cannot see what is happening, you cannot feel how you are wasting your life.[1]
> I don't want you to become Christians—that is useless, that is a lie.[2]

New Ager Benjamin Creme, who hopes to introduce the new Christ to the world in the near future, dismisses Christianity with these words:

> To my way of thinking, the Christian Churches have released into the world a view of the Christ which is impossible for modern people to accept: as the one and only Son of God, sacrificed by a loving Father to save us from the results of our sins—a blood sacrifice, straight out of the old Jewish dispensation.[3]

Alice Bailey, late founder of Lucis Trust (one of the larger offshoots from Theosophy) and former mentor of the abovementioned Benjamin Creme, condemned Christianity by saying, "The church today is the tomb of the Christ and the stone of theology has been rolled to the door of the sepulchre."[4]

Theosophy, the fountainhead for many of the pantheistic religious ideas and groups popular in the West today, set the precedent for rejecting Christianity:

> [Occult philosophy] only refuses to accept any of the Gods of the so-called monotheistic religions, Gods created by man in his own image and likeness, a blasphemous and sorry caricature of the ever unknowable.[5]

Contemporary pantheism also opposes Judaism, which asserts monotheism as does Christianity, but which denies the Christian doctrine of the trinity (one God eternally existent in three eternal Persons—the Father, the Son, and the Holy Spirit).

Alice Bailey decided that there must be "the gradual dissolution of orthodox Judaism":

> a. Because of its presentation of a wrathful Jehovah, caring only for his chosen people. This is a basic evil. The Lord of the World, the God in whom we live and move and have our being, is totally otherwise.
> b. Because of its separativeness.
> c. Because it is so ancient that its teachings are largely obsolete.[6]

The popularity of pantheistic ideas in contemporary America is due to a number of influences and factors, both religious and secular, over the last 150 years. Some of the "classic" American pantheistic groups, such as Christian Science, Unity School of Christianity, and Religious Science, have common roots in a Western form of pantheism borrowed from ancient Greek philosophies and introduced into popular American thought in the early 1800's by "mental healers" like P. P. Quimby, from whom Christian Science founder Mary Baker

Eddy took the main tenets of her new religion. Most of the newer American pantheistic groups developed their doctrines from three main sources: from importations of Eastern religious ideas by such "gurus" as Rajneesh, Praphupada, and Maharishi Mahesh Yogi, and from developments of the pantheistic ideas contained in Theosophy and in *The Aquarian Gospel of Jesus the Christ*.

Contemporary Pantheism: From Levi

The Aquarian Gospel of Jesus the Christ is a book which has enjoyed great popularity among various pantheistic groups in the United States for close to a hundred years. Along with the writings and teachings of Theosophy, this book is one of the two sources of the popular contemporary American pantheistic groups. It purports to be a record of the entire life of Christ, including the 18 years of his youth and young adulthood which are not discussed in the Bible. According to the *Aquarian Gospel*, Jesus Christ spent this period of time in Tibet, learning from the Eastern "Masters." The message of the book was "dictated" to author Levi (Levi H. Dowling) from the "Akashic Records." The dictation was accomplished through what the Bible condemns as mediumship, or communication from "familiar spirits." In occultism, this practice is often called "automatic writing." The Akashic records are not long-lost ancient manuscripts, but instead are the "universal mind" of pantheism:

> Akasha is a Sanskrit word, and means "Primary substance," that out of which all things are formed.... This philosophy recognizes the fact that all primordial substance is spirit.... This primal substance is not relegated to any particular part of the universe, but is everywhere present. It is in very fact the "Universal Mind" of which our metaphysicians speak.[7]

The *Aquarian Gospel* denies monotheism, teaching instead pantheism; denies the biblical doctrine of the Trinity, teaching instead triple attributes of one all-inclusive Substance; and denies the unique deity and humanity of Jesus Christ, teaching instead a Jesus with gnostic as well as occult and Eastern qualities. This book is also decidedly antichristian and anti-Judaistic. Its rejection of Judaism is expressed as follows:

> A superstitious people are the Jews. They have a faith that they have borrowed from the idol worshippers of other lands, that at the end of every year they may heap all their sins upon the head of some man set apart to bear their sins.[8]

Contemporary Pantheism: From Theosophy

The Theosophical Society was founded in 1875 by Madame Helena Petrovna Blavatsky (1831-1891) and her less-well-remembered cohort, Colonel H. S. Olcott. Of Russian descent, Blavatsky traveled the world for over 20 years seeking spiritual enlightenment. She studied spiritualism (attempted communication with the spirits of those who have died) and other occult practices. She finally believed that she found spiritual enlightenment in the East. Her wanderings throughout the East, especially in India and Tibet, revolutionized her religious and spiritual outlook. She completely abandoned her Christian faith and discarded Western philosophy.

Blavatsky instead embraced some of the most significant teachings of the Hindu Scriptures, the Vedas, including belief in pantheism, reincarnation, Yoga, karma, and the existence of a separate realm of reality from which the "Brotherhood of the Great White Lodge" occasionally communicate to properly receptive human beings, imparting to them the wisdom of the ages. To these Eastern ideas she added various occult practices, including automatic writing, where an individual is "possessed" by a spirit (one of the Brotherhood), who then dictates a message of revelation which the individual writes down. That Blavatsky combined a number of teachings from different sources is noted by world-religions expert Geoffrey Parrinder, who said, "It is certainly eclectic and claims to combine the wisdom of all ages and religions, with special revelations from 'Occult Mahatmas' in Tibet."[9]

Professor Dr. Johannes Aagaard describes the syncretistic* nature of Theosophy, noting that the Eastern pantheistic influences also attempt such a marriage of divergent ideas:

> Syncretism from a Christian viewpoint is only possible when Christ no longer remains at the center, but is seen as one of a number of living masters and religious saints. Syncretism in this meaning has become very popular in a series of modern syncretist movements, beginning during the last third of the 19th Century and reaching its climax in the period after World War II.
>
> Modern syncretist movements consist of two mainstreams: 1) The western occult tradition, which has developed as a mix of all sorts of religious attitudes and concepts, all centering around mind power and mind control. This main stream consists of various sub-streams, of which the Theosophical, Rosicrucian, and overtly occult syncretisms are the most important. 2) The Oriental movements, which have developed as off-shoots from mainly Hindu expressions and have the usual Indian characteristics. They do, however, often mix with the western syncretist trends and create various eclectic systems, often with gnostic characteristics.[10]

After Blavatsky's death, in 1891, some infighting for control of the fledgling organization diluted its growth and effectiveness until strong central leadership was reestablished by

---

* Syncretism is the attempt to combine or reconcile differing beliefs, especially in religion or philosophy.

one of Blavatsky's most ardent disciples, Annie W. Besant. Her writings, coupled with those of Blavatsky, form the basis of modern Theosophy's teachings.

Having briefly reviewed the main sources of contemporary pantheism, let us explore the teachings and aims of modern pantheism in its relentless attack on the Christian God.

Differences Between Theism and Pantheism

Pantheism attacks the Christian view of God by denying the distinction between the Creator and his creation. The following chart shows the distinctions between the two world views and provides the basis for our understanding of pantheism's attack on the Christian God.

THEISM	PANTHEISM
God is beyond universe.	God is universe.
God is distinct from universe	God is same as universe.
God made universe out of nothing.	God made universe out of himself.
God created all that is.	God is all that is.
Supernatural is beyond natural.	Supernatural is within natural.
Universe had beginning.	Universe is eternal.
Man is like God.	Man is God.
God is to universe as painter is to painting.	God is to universe as ocean is to water drops in it.

God Is Beyond the Universe

When Christians say that God is beyond the universe, we mean that the universe does not and cannot contain or encompass God. God is not identified in any way with the substance of the universe. The Bible asserts the supremacy of the Creator over the creation in many places, including Acts 17:24,25, where the apostle Paul declared to the unbelieving philosophers, "The God who made the world and all things in it, since He is Lord of heaven and earth, does not dwell in temples made with hands; neither is He served by human hands, as though He needed anything, since He Himself gives to all life and breath and all things."

God Is Distinct from the Universe

When we say that God is distinct from the universe, we mean that there is an essential difference between the being of God and the substance of the universe and everything in it. The pantheists confuse the essence of God with the essence of the universe, a belief condemned in Romans 1:20,23,24:

> For since the creation of the world His invisible
> attributes, His eternal power and divine nature, have
> been clearly seen, being understood through what
> has been made, so that they are without excuse....
> [They] exchanged the glory of the incorruptible God
> for an image in the form of corruptible man and
> of birds and four-footed animals and crawling crea-
> tures. Therefore God gave them over in the lusts of
> their hearts to impurity, that their bodies might be
> dishonored among them.

God Made the Universe Out of Nothing

Since pantheism identifies God with the universe and sees no essential distinction between God and the universe, pantheism also denies that God made the universe out of nothing. Instead, pantheism teaches that God made the universe out of himself. This contradicts the clear teaching of Scripture, which is that God made the universe out of nothing. Romans 4:17 links God's life-giving power with His creative power, saying, "God, who gives life to the dead and calls into being that which does not exist."

God Created All That Is

God is not part of what he has created, and nothing has come into existence that he did not create. He created the universe and everything in it. Revelation 4:11 records the praises offered to God on his throne in heaven, and those praises testify to his creative power:

> Worthy art Thou, our Lord and our God, to receive glory and honor and power; for Thou didst create all things, and because of Thy will they existed, and were created.

Jesus Christ is proclaimed in many Scriptures as this only true God, the Creator of the universe, distinct in personality but one in essence with his Father and the Holy Spirit. The apostle John's Gospel opens with a proclamation of Christ's deity and creative power:

> In the beginning was the Word, and the Word was with God, and the Word was God. He was in the beginning with God. All things came into being by Him, and apart from Him nothing came into being that has come into being (John 1:1-3).

The Supernatural Is Beyond the Natural

God has ordered the universe and established the laws of nature (Isaiah 40), but as the Lord of the universe, God can and does on occasion act *in* the universe from *beyond* the universe. Pantheism denies this, asserting that, since God is identified with the universe, by definition he cannot act from outside the universe. In other words, pantheists define miracles out of existence. (As we shall see in the next chapter, atheism also denies miracles, often through the same kind of ruse— defining them out of existence.)

The Bible contains hundreds of historical references to events which could not have been caused naturally but which are instead evidences of God's supernatural, or miraculous, intervention in the world. The disciples described God's miraculous intervention as "Thou dost extend Thy hand to heal, and signs and wonders take place through the name of Thy holy servant Jesus" (Acts 4:30).

The Universe Had a Beginning

The universe is not eternal. Only God is eternal. The universe had a beginning, and God was the Being who caused the universe to come into existence. Genesis 1:1 reminds us, "In the beginning God created the heavens and the earth." How did God create the universe? It was not out of his own substance, as pantheism would assert, but out of nothing, and by his power: "God, who gives life to the dead and calls into being that which does not exist" (Romans 4:17). Psalm 33:6 declares, "By the word of the Lord the heavens were made, and by the breath of His mouth all their host."

Man Is Like God

Man is not divine. He is not God or any part of God, both concepts which can be termed pantheistic. On the contrary, the Bible teaches that God *created* man, and that man is *like* God, but is not God himself. Genesis 1:26 records God's statement concerning the nature of man: "Let Us make man in Our image, according to Our likeness; and let them rule over the fish of the sea and over the birds of the sky and over the cattle and over all the earth, and over every creeping thing that creeps on the earth." God is unique: There is none like him, including man: "I am God, and there is no other; I am God, and there is no one like Me" (Isaiah 46:9).

God Is to the Universe As a Painter
Is to His Painting

God is not consumed by the universe, and God does not

consume the universe. There is an eternal and essential distinction between God, the Creator of all things, and the universe, which is created. Pantheism sees no ultimate essential distinction between God and the universe. However, the Bible declares, "By faith we understand that the worlds were prepared by the word of God, so that what is seen was not made out of things which are visible" (Hebrews 11:3).

The creation *reflects* God's creative power and glory, but the creation is not divine. Prophetical passages in the Bible describe God's creative acts metaphorically, picturing for us God's "artist" relationship to the world:

> [God] has measured the waters in the hollow of
> His hand, and marked off the heavens by the span,
> and calculated the dust of the earth by the measure, and weighed the mountains in a balance, and
> the hills in a pair of scales (Isaiah 40:12).

From this brief discussion, we can see that there is no way that Christian theism and pantheism can be compatible. It is not possible for theism and pantheism to be reconciled. With a firm biblical foundation, let us turn now to a review and evaluation of pantheism's central teachings.

Pantheism Sees God As All and All As God

Pantheism affirms that God is all, and all is God. God is ultimately indescribable and unknowable. New Age writer Benjamin Creme said, "To me God is the sum total of all that exists in the whole of the manifested and unmanifested universe."[11] Another New Age pantheist, David Spangler, quoted "God" describing himself this way:

> I am timeless and infinite. There is no place that
> knows me not. There is no time when I have not
> expressed what I am. I am the root of you, I am
> the stem of you, the flowering and the seed that goes

forth. I am all that you are. You will receive my
energy and it shall dwell within you and make you
one.[12]

Hinduism is the largest religious body which embraces
pantheism. The Hindu Swami Brabhavanada described the
"All" (Brahman) this way:

Him [Brahman] the eye does not see, nor the ton-
gue express, nor the mind grasp. Him we neither
know nor are able to teach. Different is he from the
known, and. . . from the unknown. He truly knows
Brahman who knows him as beyond knowledge; he
who thinks that he knows, knows not. The ignorant
think that Brahman is known, but the wise know
him to be beyond knowledge.[13]

The pantheistic God is not even personal: "It" is not a being
or a person. As David Spangler said, "It is not a Being; it is
not a personality; it is not the Christ. It is not God. It incor-
porates and is blended with the essence of many Beings and
ultimately of all Beings."[14]

Pantheism's God Is a Blend of Opposites

In fact, the pantheistic God is a blending of opposites. Luke
Skywalker's pantheistic Force combines both a "dark side"
and a "light side." It combines the yin/yang opposites of the
Zen Buddhist's Tao. As actress and reincarnationist Shirley
MacLaine put it, God also combines "polarities of positive
and negative, yin and yang, or as scientists refer to it today,
'quarks.' "[15]
The pantheistic God typically and irrationally combines the
opposites of good and evil. Star Wars creator George Lucas
said, "There is a God and there is both a Good side and a
Bad side [of God]."[16]
Since the pantheistic God combines opposites such as good

and evil, it can be called by any name anyone chooses to give it. New Age writer Alice Bailey stated:

> That central Reality [God] can be called by any name that man may choose according to his mental or emotional bend, racial tradition, and heritage, for it cannot be defined or conditioned by names.[17]

The pantheistic God combines good and evil, evil and good. Even the evil villain of Star Wars, Darth Vader, has some good in him. Luke Skywalker exclaimed of Vader, "There's good in him, I've felt it."[18]

The God of the Bible has absolutely no evil or darkness in him. In fact, the Bible tells us, "God is light, and in Him is no darkness at all" (1 John 1:5). God is absolutely holy as no created thing can ever be holy. The Hebrew prophet Habakkuk observed of God, "Your eyes are too pure to look on evil; you cannot tolerate wrong" (Habakkuk 1:13 NIV). Isaiah pronounced God's judgment on those who would try to confuse good and evil: "Woe to those who call evil good, and good evil" (Isaiah 5:20).

Pantheism Seeks Truth Through Emotions

Pantheism can combine opposites with little trouble because pantheism is not devised or accepted through reason or logic. On the contrary, pantheists believe that truth can be known only through the emotions or feelings. Both atheism and pantheism seek to destroy theism, but while many atheists claim that theism is *not* rational, and therefore wrong, many pantheists claim that theism *is* rational, and therefore wrong!

Star Wars' George Lucas admitted that his philosophy of life for determining what is true or right is based on a mystical feeling rather than on reason, logic, or critical evaluation. In his biography, Lucas recounted:

> The accident made me more aware of myself and

my feelings. I began to trust my instincts. I had the
feeling that I should go to college, and I did. I had
the same feeling later that I should go into film
school, even though everybody thought I was nuts.
I had the same feeling when I decided to make *Star
Wars*, when even my friends told me I was crazy.
There are just things that have to be done, and I feel
as if I have to do them.[19]

Pantheists refuse to trust reason; they only trust feelings.
According to Zen Buddhist spokesman T. D. Suzuki, one must
"transcend the intellect, sever yourself from the understanding, and directly penetrate deep into the identity of the Buddha-
mind; outside of this there are no realities."[20]

Pantheism Sees the Physical World As Transitory and/or Illusory

If our senses and reason are not to be trusted, then what
is the physical, material world for pantheists? It is, at best,
transitory (maya), not as "real" as "Absolute Being," or
"God." At worst, especially in many Westernized forms of
pantheism, the physical world doesn't really exist at all: It is
an illusion.

Christian Science a is Western cult which embraces many
Eastern ideas, including pantheism. Its founder, Mary Baker
Eddy, declared, "God is spirit, mind, immaterial.... God is
All-in-All...nothing is matter."[21] Levi, the "spirit master"
who dictated the *Aquarian Gospel*, put these words into Jesus'
mouth:

And Jesus said, Man is the truth and falsehood
strangely mixed.
Man is the Breath made flesh; so truth and falsehood are conjoined in him; and then they strive, and
naught goes down and man as truth abides.
Again Lamaas asked, What do you say of power?

> And Jesus said, It is a manifest; is the result of
> force; it is but naught; it is illusion, nothing more.
> Force changes not, but power changes as the ethers
> change.[22]

In other words, man's lower self is an illusion, and his higher
(immaterial) self is really divine, or God. In Levi's words:

> Man is a thought of God; all thoughts of God are
> infinite; they are not measured up by time, for things
> that are concerned with time begin and end.
> The thoughts of God are from the everlasting of
> the past unto the never ending days to come—And
> so is man, the Spirit-man.
> But man, like every other thought of God, was
> but a seed, a seed that held within itself the poten-
> cies of God, just as the seed of any plant of earth
> holds deep within itself the attributes of every part
> of that especial plant.
> So spirit-man, as seed of God, held deep within
> himself the attributes of every part of God.[23]

Pantheism Teaches That Man Is God

Since, for pantheists, God is the universe (the All), and the
universe is God, and man is part of the universe, it follows
that man is really God. Marilyn Ferguson, whose popular
report on the "New Age Movement" is contained in *The
Aquarian Conspiracy*, repeated the story of a mystic youth who
"saw God" in her sister's breast milk, concluding, "All of
a sudden I saw that she was God and the *milk* was God. I mean,
all she was doing was pouring God into God...."[24]

Actress Shirley MacLaine described in her autobiography
what she experienced of "becoming one with the All":

> My whole body seemed to float too, not only my

arms, but all of me. Slowly, slowly, I *became* the water and each tingling bubble was a component part of the water.... I felt the interconnection of my breathing with the pulse of the energy around me. The air itself seemed to pulsate. In fact, I *was* the air. I was the air, the water, the darkness, the walls, the bubbles, the candle, the wet rocks under the water, and even the sound of the rushing river outside.[25]

Pantheism Confuses Good and Evil

Pantheists are diametrically opposed to the Christian view of evil. The Bible clearly teaches that evil is a privation of good. Evil results from the deliberate disobedience to God of intelligent beings who possess free will. Evil is opposed to good. The two states have nothing in common.

On the other hand, pantheism confuses evil and good. Pantheism teaches that evil is ultimately "unreal," comes from ignorance rather than free-will choices, is not opposed to God, and is in fact part of God. The two views can be contrasted in this way:

CHRISTIAN VIEW OF EVIL	PANTHEISTIC VIEW OF EVIL
Evil is real	Evil is unreal
Evil is freely chosen	Evil is from ignorance
Evil is opposed to God	Evil is not opposed to God
Evil comes from persons	Evil comes from principles
Evil is opposed to good	Evil is not opposed to good

For example, Christian Science, one of the Western cults which adopts pantheism, teaches that evil is an illusion. Founder Mary Baker Eddy declared, "Disease, sin, evil, death, deny good, omnipotent God, Life."[26] According to Christian Science, death is "an illusion, the lie of life in matter; the unreal and untrue; the opposite of Life. Matter has no life, hence it has no real existence."[27] Hell does not really exist, teaches Christian Science, but is only "mortal belief; error"[28] and Satan is "evil; a lie; error; neither corporeality nor mind."[29] In short, for Christian Science, evil is not real; it is an error of mortal mind; it is like a dream or illusion; it only seems to exist.

Theosophy, a view which confuses evil and good, dismisses the existence of hell as a place of punishment after God's judgment, calling it "this dread superstition [that] was implanted in the minds of the poor ignorant masses, the scheme of a burning hell and souls tormented therein is purely Egyptian."[30]

Pantheism Teaches Relative Ethics

Pantheists are not without morals or ethics. Pantheism teaches ethics, but does so from a foundation completely different from that of Christian theism. Pantheistic ethical guidelines are not absolute. For the pantheist, on the ultimate level (the level at which everything is divine or God) there can be no distinction between right and wrong. The pantheist has the same confusion between right and wrong as he has between good and evil.

Alan Watts, who popularized Zen Buddhism for Westerners several years ago, declared that, for the Zen Buddhist, "the notions of right and wrong and the praise and blame of others do not disturb him."[31] Why does the Zen Buddhist appear to have no moral conscience? Because distinctions between right and wrong are only relevant in this transitory world of material existence: Those distinctions are irrelevant and in fact do not exist in the "higher" realm of pure spirit, the All of God. Right and wrong, true and false are only lower-level distinctions and dualities which disappear in a mystical state, when one becomes "one with the One and all with the All," as the ancient pantheistic Greek philosopher, Plotinus, declared.[32]

The ethics which exist for pantheists involve divine principles and cosmic forces, not personal concern and commitment.

The impersonal forces of pantheistic ethics are supposed to free a person from personal restraints of any kind, as *The Aquarian Gospel* notes: "If one is full of love he does not need commands of any kind."[33] New Ager Benjamin Creme is dogmatic concerning the impersonality of pantheistic love, calling love "a totally impersonal but all inclusive cohesive, hinging force which draws all men and all things together, and holds them together...it is the energy which makes humanity One."[34]

Christian Love in Contrast

Love as defined and taught in Christianity is categorically rejected by pantheists. Biblical love involves the free-will choices of persons who commit themselves to other persons. Biblical ethics involve obedience. Jesus said, "If you love me, keep my commandments." By contrast, Zen Buddhist Alan Watts says, "Buddhism does not share the Western view that there is a moral law, enjoined by God or by nature, which it is man's duty to obey." Moral principles are only "voluntarily assumed rules of expediency...."[35] The pantheistic aim is to progress beyond both good and bad to the all-encompassing One of divine consciousness.

A Christian Response to Pantheism

Previously I presented some of the biblical arguments against pantheism. In this section I will present some of the logical and/or philosophical arguments against pantheism.

Pantheism Is Not Rational

By its own admission, the pantheistic approach to God is not rational. It embraces logical contradictions and absurdities to which rational minds naturally object. While both atheism and pantheism are united in their aversion to theism, even atheists are prone to criticize the contradictions inherent in pantheism. Atheist Ayn Rand was critical of such subjective philosophy, noting:

> If all the manufacturers of railroad engines suddenly went irrational and began to manufacture covered wagons instead, nobody would accept the claim that this is a progressive innovation or that the iron horse has failed; and many men would step into the industrial vacuum to start manufacturing railroad engines. But when this happens in philosophy...nobody, so far, has chosen to step into the intellectual vacuum to carry on the work of man's mind.[36]

A person can persuade someone who desires to be rational and noncontradictory against pantheism by showing him the irrationality and contradictory nature of pantheism. However, not everyone desires to be rational and noncontradictory. Someone who already embraces pantheism, for example, will have bought the idea that contradiction is liberating, that irrationality is "spiritual." Such a person is not convinced by an appeal to his reason. However, such a person might be reached by approaching his view as one which, if held, refutes itself.

Pantheistic Claims Are Self-Defeating

The pantheist has rejected reasoning. However, if you ask a pantheist *why* he has rejected reason, he will give you *reasons* for it. He will claim that a person should experience God instead of think about God. But in deciding to experience God, he has thought about God. In telling you to experience God, he is thinking about God. In other words, his system self-destructs.

The pantheist claims that "ultimate reality goes beyond rational thought." But how does he know? He must have had a rational thought about ultimate reality in order to make this claim.

The pantheist claims that reality is not subject to the laws of logic. In other words, opposites can both be true at the same time in the same sense. However, the claim "Logic does not apply to reality" is itself a logical claim about reality.

The pantheist will claim that everything is divine and thus in some way true. The Christian theist will claim that only Christianity is true; everything is not true. The pantheist will counter, "Christianity is wrong: everything is true." But he has just refuted himself: If Christianity is wrong, then not everything is true. But if Christianity is true, then its claims to exclusivity are true, and pantheism is wrong. But if pantheism is wrong, then not everything is true. The pantheist becomes mired in an endlessly repeating and self-refuting argument.

Pantheists Cannot Affirm or Prove Their Position

Some pantheists try to avoid the preceding dilemma by denying that the statement "Everything is true" is a meaningful or true claim about reality. In fact, they would deny that any statements they make are true claims. They hope in this manner to avoid being charged with affirming logical or rational thought at the same time they are attempting to deny it.

However, if this is the case, then why do they attempt to evangelize for their point of view? Why dialogue? Why hold conversations? Why write books about pantheism? (Even here they dare not even think about reality, because if they *think* that *thought* does not apply to reality, then they have just used *thought* to do what they claim *thought* cannot do.) Pantheist Alan Watts thought of a clever, although not successful, response to this charge:

> Why The Book? Why not sit back and let things
> take their course? Simply that it is part of "things
> taking their course" that I write. As a human being
> it is just my nature to enjoy and share philosophy.

> I do this in the same way that some birds are
> eagles and some doves, some flowers lilies and some
> roses.[37]

In short, Watts defends pantheism because of his animal
instincts. He is no more a conscious, intelligent person possessing free will than is a rock that does a good job of being
a rock. Pantheism entices followers by promising them divinity.
But pantheism traps followers by reducing them to the impersonal stuff of the universe.

By contrast, the biblical God created humans in his own
image, possessing intelligence, emotion, and free will. Human
dignity is both promised and confirmed by the Bible:

> When I consider Thy heavens, the work of Thy
> fingers, the moon and the stars, which Thou hast
> ordained, what is man, that Thou dost take thought
> of him? And the son of man, that Thou dost care
> for him? Yet Thou hast made him a little lower than
> [the angels], and dost crown him with glory and
> majesty! Thou dost make him to rule over the works
> of Thy hands; Thou hast put all things under his
> feet.... O Lord, our Lord, how majestic is Thy
> name in all the earth! (Psalm 8:3-6,9).

Pantheism's View of God Is Inconsistent

Pantheism asserts that God is an eternal, changeless, infinite
being. However, it also claims that man goes through a *changing* process of enlightenment through which he discovers that
he himself is this unchanging God!

But if man really is God, then he must be changeless. If he
changes, he either cannot be God or else God must be changing.
The fact that a man changes by "coming to realize" that he
is God proves that he is not God.

In order to assert a consistent view of God, the pantheist

must choose one of the following options: 1) God is changing, and man changes in becoming or realizing that he is God; 2) God is changeless, and man is not God; 3) God is changeless, and man is God, and man is always and knows always that he is God. However, by choosing options one or three, the pantheist makes himself vulnerable to a host of other logical and philosophical problems, and by choosing option two the pantheist denies pantheism!

Pantheism Has No Adequate Explanation for Human Error

Pantheism cannot assert the infallibility of God's mind and at the same time account for the fallibility of man's mind, if man is really divine. Christian author C. S. Lewis posed and answered the dilemma this way:

> The traditional doctrine that I am a creature to whom God has given reason but who is distinct from God seems to me much more philosophical than the theory that what appears to be my thinking is only God's thinking through me. On the latter view it is very difficult to explain what happens when I think correctly but reach a false conclusion because I have been misinformed about facts. Why God—who presumably knows the real facts—should be at the pains to think one of His perfectly rational thoughts through a mind in which it is bound to produce error, I do not understand. Nor indeed do I understand why, if all "my" valid thinking is really God's, He should either Himself mistake it for mine or cause me to mistake it for mine. It seems much more likely that human thought is not God's but God-kindled.[38]

Pantheism Has No Adequate Explanation for Evil

According to pantheism, evil does not exist. But why does

it seem so real? Where did this illusion come from? Why is it so universal? Why is it that when I sit on a tack and it punctures my skin, I dislike what I only think I feel?

Humorist Mark Twain poked fun at what seemed to him a ridiculous idea: Nothing exists but divine Mind. He recounted this dialogue he had with a "mental practitioner" who was a pantheist:

> "Nothing exists but Mind?"
>
> "Nothing," she answered. "All else is substance-less, all else is imaginary."
>
> I gave her an imaginary check, and now she is suing me for substantial dollars. It looks inconsistent.[39]

Pantheism Destroys the Distinction Between Good and Evil

As pantheists readily admit, they believe that there is no real difference between good and evil "on the highest level of consciousness." The absurd consequences of this are vividly illustrated by the late Francis Schaeffer:

> One day I was talking to a group of people in the digs of a young South African in Cambridge. Among others, there was present a young Indian who was of Sikh background but a Hindu by religion. He started to speak strongly against Christianity, but did not really understand the problems of his own beliefs. So I said, "Am I not correct in saying that on the basis of your system, cruelty and non-cruelty are ultimately equal, that there is no intrinsic difference between them?" He agreed...the student in whose room we met, who had clearly understood the implications of what the Sikh had admitted, picked up his kettle of boiling water with

which he was about to make tea, and stood with it steaming over the Indian's head. The man looked up and asked him what he was doing and he said, with a cold yet gentle finality, "There is no difference between cruelty and non-cruelty." Thereupon the Hindu walked out into the night.[40]

Pantheism Encourages Indifference to Human Suffering

Very little compassion flows out of a system whose goal is to disengage a person from the physical world and into the mystical world. The horrible social conditions of India testify to this fact. Belief in reincarnation and the retributive law of karma flow directly from this pantheistic assumption.

If a person is suffering in this life because of evil done in a previous life, then any alleviation of that suffering will interfere with the person's slow "evolution" out of evil and into "nirvana," or the heavenly bliss of unconsciousness in the divine mind.

Most of the social compassion manifest in India today is due either directly or indirectly to the influence of Christianity on that country. Christianity has inspired human compassion around the world over the centuries. Christian love inspired William Wilberforce to overthrow the repressive British slave labor practices. Christian love motivated George Mueller to found orphanages for homeless children. Christian love motivated Jean-Henri Dunant to found the Red Cross. Untold thousands of hospitals, rescue missions, and social-action organizations are eloquent testimony to the positive influence of Christian ethics. Pantheism encourages indifference to human suffering.

Conclusion

Pantheism is unsuccessful in its attack on the Christian God. It is contrary to the Bible, contrary to reason, contrary to common sense, contrary to reality, and contrary to human conscience. Like atheism, pantheism cannot provide an adequate world view. It must be abandoned for the reasonableness and truth of Christian theism.

CHAPTER 5

Naturalism Attacks Miracles

Theistic belief means belief in a God beyond the world who created the world and who, from time to time, supernaturally intervenes in the world. One of the unique claims of Christian theism is that God can and does involve himself personally with people.

Atheism denies any supernatural intervention in the world, declaring that there is no God "out there" who "acts here." The universe, or nature, is "the whole show." There is nothing in existence which is not the material universe or which does not derive from the material universe.

Pantheism also denies any supernatural intervention in the world, but for a different reason. Pantheism identifies God with the universe, and so God is not "out there," sometimes "acting here." Instead, God *is* the universe, God *is* the "here." Any divine actions are the actions of the universe as his expression or extension. They are not *super* (more than) natural. They are just natural.

Miracles Are Necessary to Christianity

There can be no compatibility between Christianity and any kind of naturalism, whether atheistic or pantheistic. On the

contrary, the miraculous is an essential feature of Christian
theism. Through the supernatural intervention of God in this
world, our redemption from sin and death was accomplished:
"God was in Christ reconciling the world to Himself" (2
Corinthians 5:19). The resurrection of Jesus Christ from the
dead is the pivotal act of human history, and the pivotal miracle
of divine action in the world. The apostle Paul wrote that there
would be no Christianity if there were no resurrection from
the dead. In fact, there would be no hope for mankind at all
without the miracle of the resurrection:

> If Christ has not been raised, then our preaching
> is vain; your faith also is vain. Moreover we are even
> found to be false witnesses of God, because we wit-
> nessed against God that He raised Christ, whom He
> did not raise...and if Christ has not been raised,
> your faith is worthless; you are still in your sins....
> If we have hoped in Christ in this life only, we are
> of all men most to be pitied (1 Corinthians 15:14-19).

Any attack on the possibility and existence of miracles is
an attack upon historical Christianity.

Christianity is Historical

Christianity is not just some myth which gave empty solace
to primitive people. Christianity is rooted and grounded in
history. There have been detractors through the years, many
of them naturalists, who have attempted to reduce Christianity
to emotional wishing or myth-making and Christ to a simple
man transformed by legend into a god. However, the claims
of Christianity, including the resurrection of Jesus Christ, pass
every reasonable and objective historical test. The Gospel writer
Luke was adamant: The story of Jesus Christ which he
recorded was absolute and verified truth.

> Inasmuch as many have undertaken to com-
> pile an account of the things accomplished among
> us, just as those who from the beginning were

eyewitnesses and servants of the word have handed them down to us, it seemed fitting for me as well, having *investigated everything carefully from the beginning*, to write it out for you in consecutive order, most excellent Theophilus, so that you might know the *exact truth* about the things you have been taught (Luke 1:1-4).

The apostle Peter echoed Luke's claim, noting, "For we did not follow cleverly devised tales when we made known to you the power and coming of our Lord Jesus Christ, but we were *eyewitnesses* of His majesty" (2 Peter 1:16). The apostle Paul appealed to the historical verifiability of the resurrection of Jesus Christ when he proclaimed the gospel. For example, he challenged his captors with the historical truth claims of Christianity, saying, "I utter words of sober truth. For the king knows about these matters, and I speak to him also with confidence, since I am persuaded that none of these things escape his notice; for this has not been done in a corner" (Acts 26:25,26).

Christianity is provable by history. And Christianity is founded upon miracles, the greatest of all being the resurrection of Jesus Christ from the dead.

Naturalism Attacks Miracles

What do we mean when we say "naturalism"? Naturalism is basically the idea that all existence and all events are part of and are bound by the natural (material) world. (First we will deal with naturalism unrelated to any religious ideas or convictions, then with "religious" pantheistic naturalism.) For the naturalist, there is no possibility of a miracle because a miracle would have its origin outside the universe. However, if the universe is all that exists, then there is nothing outside the universe which could generate a miracle.

In the following pages we will review and answer the most important of the modern naturalistic attacks on miracles. Not

all of the naturalists quoted are confirmed atheists: Some are
agnostics, some are skeptics, and some are pantheists.
However, all of them are committed to naturalism and thus
reject any possibility of miracles.

The Dutch Jewish philosopher Benedict de Spinoza (Baruch
de Spinoza) (1632-1677) was one of the most influential early
thinkers to assert absolute naturalism. God, to Spinoza, is
everything that exists and everything that is coming into being.
He is properly a pantheist, and his naturalism discounts any
possibility of miracles. Spinoza declared, "Nothing, then,
comes to pass in nature in contravention to her universal
laws...."[1]

The Scottish philosopher and skeptic David Hume
(1711-1776) spoke of "the absolute impossibility or miraculous
nature of the events...a miracle is a violation of the laws of
nature," which have been established by "unalterable
experience." Thus, asserts Hume, "Nothing is esteemed a
miracle if it ever happened in the common course of nature."[2]

Immanuel Kant (1724-1804) was another philosopher who
was a skeptic, and his teachings heavily influenced much of
the later eighteenth- and nineteenth-century philosophies. He
contended that "miracles must be admitted as...not at all compatible with reason...." Instead, miracles are "nothing but
natural effects...."[3]

The father of American "progressive education," John
Dewey (1859-1952), asserted that belief in God and supernaturalism had a negative effect on people, and that "dependence upon an external power is the counterpart of surrender
of human endeavor." He stated, "The contention of an
increasing number of persons is that depreciation of natural
social values has resulted, both in principle and in fact, from
reference of their origin and significance to supernatural
source."[4]

British biologist and author Sir Julian Huxley (1887-1977),
grandson of Darwinist T. H. Huxley (1825-1895), claimed in
1957 that discoveries in science "not only make possible, but
necessitate, a naturalistic hypothesis, in which there is no room

for the supernatural...." and that "the supernatural is being swept out of the universe in the flood of new knowledge of what is natural."[5]

Tracing naturalistic thought from the seventeenth century through today, we find that naturalists consistently reject any possibility of miracles. One popular atheistic defense by contemporary atheist author George Smith is consistent in this stream, asserting that miracles are absolutely impossible:

> There is no such possibility, even in principle. Naturalism has the priority over supernaturalism, not because it is the more economical of two explanations, but because it is the only framework in which explanation is possible.[6]

How can the naturalists be so dogmatic in their denial of the supernatural? Because they have assumed that the material universe is all that exists, and therefore have defined miracles out of existence! If there is no God—if the universe is all that exists—then of course there could be no miracles. However, the universe is not all that exists, and God, who is outside the universe and created the universe, can and does intervene in his universe in miraculous ways. To obtain a better understanding of the roots of naturalism, let us look more closely at the development of this package called naturalism.

The Roots of Modern Naturalism

Thomas Hobbes

The roots of modern naturalism go back at least as far as the English philosopher Thomas Hobbes (1588-1679). Hobbes applied the naturalistic method of modern physics to the study of mankind. He believed that all knowledge is based on experience. His naturalism was so strict that he explained everything in terms of mechanical causal explanations, even going so far as to deny human free will. For Hobbes, natural determinism prevails in everything that happens. Because of his thoroughgoing naturalism, he rejected all possibility of miracles, surmising that people like to believe in supernatural causes because of "the want of curiosity to search natural causes."[7]

Benedict Spinoza

Spinoza was a generation later than Hobbes, although Hobbes ultimately outlived Spinoza. Spinoza's theories on naturalism have been, over the years, probably more popular than Hobbes', and his attacks on miracles have been more quoted, borrowed, reworded, and modified countless times over the intervening centuries. This is how Spinoza argued that miracles were impossible:

> Whatever comes to pass, comes to pass according to laws and rules which involved eternal necessity and truth; nature, therefore, always observes laws and rules which involve eternal necessity and truth, although they may not all be known to us, and therefore she keeps a fixed and immutable order.[8]

"Nature," said Spinoza, "follows a fixed and immutable order."[9] Spinoza was forced by his own system to reject the miracles of the Bible, saying, "When Scripture describes an event as accomplished by God or God's will, we must understand merely that it was in accordance with the law and order of nature...." He further asserted that we cannot believe, in the case of biblical miracles, as some people do, "that nature had for a season ceased to act, or that her order was temporarily interrupted."[10]

Spinoza scoffed at the Bible's description of miracles, saying that it was—

> plain that all the events narrated in Scripture came to pass naturally, and are referred directly to God

because Scripture, as we have shown, does not aim at explaining things by their natural causes, but only at narrating what *appeals to the popular imagination.*[11]

David Hume

Probably no other naturalistic thinker has had as great or consistent an effect on modern naturalism than David Hume. Many people who reject the possibility of miracles have been taught naturalism in school as it was formulated and espoused by Hume. Hume dealt with miracles by explaining them out of existence. He so defined terms as to effectively preclude all miracles.

What was Hume's most important "proof" against miracles? It was *uniform* experience. Hume appealed to science. Doesn't science explain the world around us in terms of cause and effect? Doesn't science assume that natural law is inviolate and that, if the causes could be discerned, all of the effects would flow naturally from those causes? Where, then, is room for miracles? Nowhere. According to Hume, one cannot have both science and miracles; one can have *either* science or miracles. The two, for Hume, are completely incompatible.

Hume decided that a miracle was a break in natural law. But natural law, he said, was "law" because it was *never* broken or violated. Well, if it has *never* been broken or violated, then a miracle could *never* have happened. He said:

> [There must] be a uniform experience against every miraculous event, otherwise the event would not merit that appellation. And as a uniform experience amounts to a proof, there is here a direct and full *proof*, from the nature of the fact, against the existence of *any* miracle, nor can such a proof be destroyed or the miracle rendered credible but by an opposite proof which is superior.[12]

The common argument against miracles, taken from Hume, and modified over the years, most notably by the contemporary philosopher Antony Flew (Professor of Philosophy, University of Reading), can be summarized as follows:

1. Miracles are by nature particular and unrepeatable.
2. Natural events are by nature general and repeatable.
3. Now in practice, the evidence for the general and repeatable is always greater than that for the particular and unrepeatable.
4. Therefore, in practice, the evidence will *always* be greater against miracles than for them.

In brief, miracles are unscientific because they are improbable, unrepeatable, and unique. Science, on the other hand, deals with probabilities and regularities. There cannot be any miracles. Let us turn now to a critique of arguments against miracles, including a critique of the argument above.

Answers to Atheistic Naturalism

Since miracles are at the heart of the Christian view of God and the world, it is essential to answer the atheistic naturalism we have just reviewed. We will answer these naturalists from four major arguments in the areas of 1) the existence of God; 2) logic; 3) probability; and 4) the limits of scientific observation.

The Existence of God

If God exists, then miracles are possible. Naturalism argues that since the universe is all that exists, there couldn't have been a God who performs miracles. The key to the naturalistic argument is its first assertion: *since* the universe is all that exists. But nowhere have the naturalists proved that assertion:

They have never proved that the universe is all that exists. God exists outside the universe, is the universe's cause and Sustainer, and sometimes acts in the universe, in miracles.

Even most atheists will admit that they cannot disprove God's existence. What they assert instead is that none of the theistic arguments are convincing to them. However, this does not eliminate the possibility of God's existence. Popular agnostic Bertrand Russell (1872-1970) admitted that he was "at a loss to find conclusive arguments" against God's existence.[13] The Cosmos television series host Carl Sagan admitted, "There can, of course, be no disproof of the existence of God."[14]

As long as God's existence is possible, then miracles are possible. Once we acknowledge that there could be a supernatural Creator and Sustainer of the world (nature), then there is no way to lock him out of his universe.

Logic

Few naturalists offer any logical proof for their naturalism. Instead, they simply assume its truth. Those who do argue for naturalism usually argue in a circle. Their argument usually goes like this:

1. Natural law exists.
2. Natural law is unalterable.
3. Miracles alter natural law.
4. Therefore, miracles are impossible.

That argument looks sound, but it has a fatal flaw. How do we know that each of the first two assumptions is true? Well, we have to investigate the evidence. Is there any evidence that would lead us to think that natural law is *not* unalterable? Yes—any evidence for a miracle, which is an unusual, infrequent alteration of natural law. However, if one assumes without proof that natural law is unalterable, then any evidence which the Christian theist brings up in support of miracles is discarded as unreliable by definition. Christian writer C. S.

Lewis criticized this view well when he said:

> Now of course we must agree with Hume that if there is absolutely "uniform experience" against miracles, if in other words they have never happened, why then they never have. Unfortunately we know the experience against them to be uniform only if we know that all the reports of them are false. And we can know all the reports to be false only if we know already that miracles have never occurred. In fact, we are arguing in a circle.[15]

Probability

One of the arguments for naturalism is that the intelligent person should always base his belief on the highest probability. Since a miracle is rare, it is highly improbable. Since miracles are always highly improbable, the intelligent person should never believe in them.

But there is an important mistake in this argument, for, given sufficient evidence, we *should* believe the improbable. The odd or unusual sometimes actually happens. A hole-in-one in golf is unusual, but this does not mean that we should never believe it when the evidence shows that it happened. The odds for getting a perfect bridge hand in the card game of that name are 1 in 635,013,559,600. But despite these incredible odds, some people have been dealt a perfect bridge hand! When the evidence shows that such a thing has happened, the intelligent person does not reject this unusual fact because it is "improbable," but accepts the evidence and thus the act.

The odds against someone surviving a fall from an airplane at 12,000 feet when his parachute fails are very slim. However, it did happen to Air Force pilot Thomas Smoke, who survived such a fall in 1961 in Little Rock, Arkansas. In fact, Smoke landed in a residential yard and didn't even break his legs! Such an event is highly improbable and unusual, but it did happen.

The foolishness of the probability argument against naturalism was illustrated by the English logician Richard Whately (1787-1863), who wrote a short satire of David Hume's skepticism against miracles entitled *Historic Doubts Relative to Napoleon Buonaparte*. Whately argued that if Hume were right about disbelieving the improbable, then no one should believe the highly unusual exploits of Napoleon Bonaparte. Whately concluded his satire by pointing out that naturalists who use this argument against miracles are not willing to use it consistently:

> If after all has that has been said, they cannot bring themselves to doubt of the existence of Napoleon Buonaparte, they must at least acknowledge that they do not apply to that question the same plan of reasoning which they have made use of in others, and they are consequently bound in reason and in honesty to renounce it altogether.[16]

The Limits of Scientific Observation

The evidence for what is regular and/or repeated is not always greater than the evidence for what is unusual and/or unrepeated. However, contemporary scientists often object to miracles because they are unrepeated singularities, and as such they cannot be repeated for scientific observation and verification.

However, there are many things we believe to be true which cannot be verified by scientific observation. In fact, the same scientists who *reject* miracles because they are not scientifically verifiable *accept* the scientifically unverifiable theory of the "Big Bang" origin of the universe.

These scientists argue that the universe came into being billions of years ago with a great explosion that no one was there to observe and which has never been repeated since. The "Big Bang" is an unobserved, unrepeated singularity which many astronomers believe is supported overwhelmingly by "the evidence." Contemporary astronomer Dr. Robert Jastrow gave a splendid explanation of this scientific predicament:

> Consider the enormity of the problem. Science has proven that the Universe exploded into being at a certain moment. It asks, What cause produced this effect? Who or what put the matter and energy into the Universe? Was the Universe created out of nothing, or was it gathered together out of pre-existing materials? And science cannot answer these questions, because, according to the astronomers, in the first moments of its existence the Universe was compressed to an extraordinary degree, and consumed by the heat of a fire beyond human imagination. The shock of that instant must have destroyed every particle of evidence that could have yielded a clue to the cause of the great explosion. An entire world, rich in structure and history, may have existed before our Universe appeared; but if it did, science cannot tell what kind of world it was. A sound explanation may exist for the explosive birth of our Universe, but if it does, science cannot find out what the explanation is. The scientist's pursuit of the past ends in the moment of creation.[17]

But if the evidence leads back to a point of creation, then why not a Creator? It is scientific to seek causes for events, and the only adequate cause (not scientifically testable, but reasonable and consistent) for the creation of the world is a supernatural cause. Scientists bring us to the brink of the supernatural, but are too bound by their own narrow system of verification to logically go beyond the brink. Jastrow noted this, saying:

> Now we would like to pursue that inquiry farther back in time, but the barrier to further progress seems insurmountable. It is not a matter of another year, another decade of work, another measurement, or another theory; at this moment it seems as though

science will never be able to raise the curtain on the mystery of creation. For the scientist who has lived by his faith in the power of reason, the story ends like a bad dream. He has scaled the mountains of ignorance; he is about to conquer the highest peak; as he pulls himself over the final rock, he is greeted by a band of theologians who have been sitting there for centuries.[18]

Scientists have a distaste for any outside interference into what they consider (wrongly) their "sovereign domain," the natural world. Nonetheless, even atheists have to admit that creation from nothing (we Christians say from nothing through the power of God) is possible. One atheist recently admitted it by saying, "Distressing as it is for an atheist such as myself to have to admit it, we have here a model for God's interference, by way of miracle, with the working out of ordinary natural processes."[19]

We can see from all that we have surveyed that atheistic naturalism cannot argue successfully against Christian theism. Let us turn now to the claims of pantheistic or "religious" naturalism.

Religious Pantheism Attacks Miracles

Atheists and pantheists differ in their interpretations of the universe. Atheists reduce all of existence ultimately to matter. Pantheists reduce all of existence ultimately to spirit. Atheists believe there is no God at all. Pantheists believe God is All. However, both atheism and pantheism attack Christian theism on a number of fronts, including the way each system attacks the Christian concept of miracles.

Atheism denies the possibility of miracles, as we have just seen, in this way: The natural (universe) is all that exists. Miracles, by definition, are caused by something or Someone outside the universe. Since that something or Someone cannot exist, miracles cannot be caused and therefore miracles are not possible.

Pantheistic Naturalism Denies Miracles

Pantheism denies the possibility of miracles, as we will see, in this way: The natural (universe), which is divine (Spirit) is all that exists. Miracles, by the Christian definition, are caused by something or Someone outside the natural. Since that something or Someone cannot exist, miracles cannot be caused and therefore miracles are not possible. However, events that Christians often call "supernatural" pantheism calls "supernormal" or "superphysical." In other words, these things actually happen, but they happen as part of the fabric of this existence, not as an intrusion into this existence from outside this existence.

Pantheists believe that there are spiritual and mystical laws which go beyond the apparent physical world. This spiritual realm is an integral part of nature (the All), and this spiritual realm is also governed by natural laws. This spiritual realm is a Force which, like Luke Skywalker's Force, for example, anyone can learn to use for his own good or bad ends.

Pantheists reject the theistic belief that there is a personal supernatural God beyond nature who can and has occasionally intervened in nature according to his own will.

Pantheism, Natural Law, and Miracles

Pantheism denies that miracles are interruptions in natural law. Pantheism sees a "miracle" as the outworking of a natural law in the spiritual or psychic realm. For example, the pantheistic *Aquarian Gospel*, purported to be a psychically obtained account of Jesus' supposed psychic training and teaching, declares, "All things result from natural law."[20] The Western pantheistic Christian Science cult founder, Mary Baker Eddy, defined a miracle as "that which is divinely natural, but must be learned humanly; a phenomenon of Science."[21] By identifying "miracles" with "natural law," the pantheists are setting the stage for their belief that anyone can be trained to use these natural laws, as Luke Skywalker was trained to use the Force.

Mary Baker Eddy said that the so-called miracles of the Bible are the accounts "of the triumph of the Spirit, Mind, over matter."[22] They are not records of supernatural intervention into the natural world.

Levi's Aquarian Jesus said, "The laws of nature are the laws of health, and he who lives according to these laws is never sick.... [The] transgression of these laws is sin, and he who sins is sick."[23]

According to pantheist Mary Baker Eddy, even the resurrection of Jesus Christ was not supernatural:

> Could it be called supernatural for the God of nature to sustain Jesus in his proof of man's truly derived power? It was a method of surgery beyond material art, but it was not a supernatural act. On the contrary, it was a divinely natural act, whereby divinity brought to humanity the understanding of the Christ-healing and revealed a method infinitely above that of human invention.[24]

The Pantheistic God and Miracles

The basis for the pantheistic attack on miracles is the nature of the pantheistic God. According to pantheism, God is nature and nature is God. Therefore there can be no God beyond nature, which is God. This tenet of pantheism was noted by New Age observer Marilyn Ferguson, who wrote:

> For years those interested in phenomena of the human mind had predicted that a breakthrough theory would emerge; that it would draw on mathematics to establish the supernatural as part of nature.[25]

Pantheists offer as evidence of the availability of this "spiritual" aspect of nature a whole host of supernormal and parapsychological events, including ESP, telepathy, clairvoyance, near-death experiences, psychic healings, and even individuals returning from the dead.

New Ager Alice Bailey did not believe in the biblical Christ. For her, Christ was "the Christ," the mystic power of God which can be appropriated by other people through the aid of "angels" pledged to the service of "the Christ." These "angels" "will train human beings in the knowledge of superhuman physics so that weight for them will be transmuted ...motion will become more rapid, speed will be accompanied by noiselessness and smoothness, and hence fatigue will be eliminated."[26]

Pantheists have even attempted to join the science of physics to pantheism and supernormal powers. An example of this strange marriage is Fritjof Capra's popular *The Tao of Physics*, in which Capra attempts to show that modern subatomic physics has come to recognize the mystical nature of the universe, a view taught for centuries by pantheists. In Capra's words:

> The basic oneness of the universe is not only the central characteristic of the mystical experience, but is also one of the most important revelations of modern physics. It becomes apparent at the atomic level and manifests itself more and more as one penetrates deeper into matter, down into the realm of subatomic particles.[27]

Pantheists typically relegate the unique miracles of Jesus Christ recorded in the Gospels to the realm of magical powers for which anyone has the potential: It is possible for anyone to progress to the level of psychic prowess to which Jesus progressed. New Ager Benjamin Creme's writings are typical of this type of theosophical influence. For example, here is what Creme wrote about "the Christ," "the Maitreya," the psychic divinity who "possessed" the man Jesus:

> He was, and still is, a Disciple of Christ and made
> the great sacrifice of giving up His body for the use
> of the Christ. By the occult process of overshadow-
> ing, the Christ, Maitreya, took over and worked
> through the body of Jesus from the Baptism
> onwards.[28]

Creme's mentor, Alice Bailey, who learned her system from
Theosophy, calls the Christ (not to be confused with the Christian and biblical Jesus Christ) "the Master of all the [occult]
Masters."[29] According to Bailey, Creme, and many other pantheists, this Christ spirit (which possessed the man Jesus) has
now been released into the world for the last 2000 years, and
its power is available to the followers of "the Christ." Creme
said, "It is this which has enabled them to perform what
at that time were called miracles, which today are called
spiritual or esoteric healing. Daily, all over the world, there
are miracles of healing performed...these miracles are
now being performed by men and women in the world all the
time."[30]

We have seen from above that 1) pantheism, like atheism,
denies the possibility of miracles; 2) pantheism denies miracles because pantheism identifies God with nature; 3) pantheism explains "miracles" as part of the psychic or spiritual
"natural world," and 4) pantheism teaches that anyone, with
proper initiation, training, etc. can perform the same "miracles" attributed in the Bible to Jesus Christ. Let us now give
a Christian response to pantheistic or "religious" naturalism.

A Christian Response
to Pantheistic Naturalism

Christians Do Not Deny the Supernormal

Christianity does not deny, as pantheists often assert, the

possibility of *any* supernormal, occult occurrences. Christians only deny that the events usually cataloged as such by pantheists have their source in the one true and living God. Such events are labeled in the Bible, especially in the Old Testament, as occult events with their sources in satanic power, not in natural or divine power. The Bible teaches that Satan is the chief angel created by God who rebelled against God, and chose to use his angelic powers for evil ends rather than for God's glory (Revelation 12:9).

According to the Bible, God created everything good (Genesis 1:31), including angels (Colossians 1:15,16) and man (Genesis 1:27,28). One of those angels was called Lucifer (Isaiah 14:12). Being lifted up with pride (1 Timothy 3:6), Lucifer said, "I will make myself like the Most High" (Isaiah 14:14). In this rebellion against God, one-third of all the angels created by God joined forces with Lucifer (Revelation 12:4). These beings are now known as Satan (or the devil) and his demons (Revelation 12:7; Matthew 25:41).

The devil and these demons (evil spirits) have unusual powers which are now "working [energizing] in the sons of disobedience" (Ephesians 2:2). By the power of Satan, his angelic followers are described as "spirits of demons, performing signs [miracles] which go out to the kings of the whole world..." (Revelation 16:14).

The Bible teaches that one day Satan will send a false Christ into the world "whose coming is in accord with the activities of Satan, with all power and signs [miracles] and false wonders" (2 Thessalonians 2:9). So great will be his occultic powers that "he performs great signs [miracles], so that he even makes fire come down out of heaven.... And he deceives those who dwell on the earth because of the signs which it is given him to perform..." (Revelation 13:13,14).

This same devil, Satan, is able to "disguise himself as an angel of light" (2 Corinthians 11:14). His servants also disguise themselves as "servants of righteousness" (v. 15). These demonic spirits will speak against the central doctrines of biblical Christianity. About them the apostle Paul warned:

But the [Holy] Spirit explicitly says that in later times some will fall away from the faith, paying attention to deceitful spirits and doctrines of demons, by means of the hypocrisy of liars seared in their own conscience as with a branding iron, men who forbid marriage and advocate abstaining from foods, which God has created to be gratefully shared in by those who believe and know the truth (1 Timothy 4:1-3).

These demonic spirits will deny that Jesus is God who has come in the flesh (John 4:1,14). Of them the apostle John said, "Who is the liar but the one who denies that Jesus is the Christ? This is the antichrist, the one who denies the Father and the Son" (1 John 2:22). John urged Christians:

Beloved, do not believe every spirit, but test the spirits to see whether they are from God, because many false prophets have gone out into the world. By this you know the Spirit of God: every spirit that confesses that Jesus Christ has come in the flesh is from God, and every spirit that does not confess Jesus is not from God; and this is the spirit of the antichrist, of which you have heard that it is coming, and now it is already in the world (1 John 4:1-3).

The Bible details exactly how to distinguish these false spirits and false miracles from the true God and his true miracles.

Biblical Miracles Versus Occultic Magic

The Scriptures set up several tests for a false prophet, even if that prophet performs unusual feats. By these tests the Christian can distinguish satanic magic from genuine divine miracles. The following chart summarizes these differences:

MIRACLE	MAGIC
Under God's control	Under man's control
Not available on command	Available on command
Supernatural power	Called a natural "mystic" power
Associated with good	Associated with evil
Associated with truth	Associated with error
Can overpower evil	Cannot overpower good
Affirms Jesus' incarnation	Denies Jesus' incarnation
Prophecies always true	Prophecies often false
Never associated with occult	Often associated with occult

These differences translate into recognizable traits which Christians can discern in association with demonic signs. The following signs are demonic and cannot be associated with miracles from the biblical God:

1. Witchcraft (Deuteronomy 18:10).
2. Fortune-telling (Deuteronomy 18:10).
3. Communicating with spirits (Deuteronomy 18:11).
4. Mediumship (Deuteronomy 18:11).
5. Divination (Deuteronomy 18:10).
6. Astrology (Deuteronomy 4:19; Isaiah 47:13-15).
7. Heresy (false teaching) (1 Timothy 4:1; 1 John 4:1,2).
8. Immorality (Ephesians 2:2,3; 2 Thessalonians 2:7).
9. Self-deification (Isaiah 14:12; Genesis 3:5).
10. Lying (John 8:44).
11. Idolatry (1 Corinthians 10:19,20).

By reflecting the pantheistic attack on Christian miracles with the list above, it is clear that pantheistic "miracles" are demonic. In fact, many pantheists admit that most of the above practices are part of their belief and practices.

Occult Magic and Fraud

Many of the "supernormal" or "miraculous" events performed by occult practitioners are not demonic or divine, but are instead actually tricks fostered as "proof" of the practitioners' "divine power." A number of performing magicians have, over the years, exposed many occultic performers as charlatans. The famous magician Houdini claimed to be able to duplicate any medium's "miracles" by natural, learned trick techniques. His exposé of mediums has become a classic refutation of the bulk of occultic events. A contemporary professional magician who is also a Christian, Danny Korem, has made a careful study of occult practices and has written a book, *The Fakers* (Here's Life Publishers), exposing the rampant fraud he discovered.

For example, let us examine the occult power claimed by Israeli "psychi" Uri Geller. The claims of Geller are astounding, and include telepathy, clairvoyance, psychic "watch repair," and psychic "metal bending," all feats performed without physically touching the items included. Yet despite numerous public and well-staged media events where Geller has displayed his amazing talents, many careful investigators are convinced that Geller is a fraud, and that his feats are accomplished by clever cheating rather than by some sort of natural psychic power.

New Science magazine, for example, recorded that "at least five people claim to have seen Geller actually cheat." Sandy MacCrae said that while Geller had diverted everyone's attention one time, "she actually saw Geller bend—by hand, not psychic powers—the large spoon."[31] Geller also claims to be able to take pictures with a camera while the lens cap is still in place. However, this dramatic feat has been duplicated by a photographer using nothing more than an extreme wide angle lense and a lense cover with a slight gap between it and the camera.[32]

Geller's most publicized Stanford Research Institute study has been criticized by experts. Dr. Joseph Hanlon declared

flatly that "the SRI paper simply does not stand up against
the mass of circumstantial evidence that Uri Geller is simply
a good magician."[33]

Even the editors of *Nature*, which published the controver-
sial SRI paper, published a disclaimer with the article:

> The referees felt that insufficient account had been
> taken of the established methodology of experimen-
> tal psychology and that in the form originally
> submitted the paper would be unlikely to be accepted
> for publication in a psychological journal on these
> grounds alone. Two referees also felt that the authors
> had not taken into account the lessons learned in
> the past by parapsychologists researching this tricky
> and complicated area.[34]

In addition, Geller's failure rate rises as the controls imposed
on him are tightened. One of Geller's "tricks" is to pick an
object from one of ten unmarked film cans. Dr. Hanlon reports
Geller's failure as follows:

> On the Merv Griffin show on US TV, Geller did
> the trick successfully, but some people thought they
> saw Geller jarring the table so that the cans would
> shake and he could tell which was heaviest. On the
> Johnny Carson Tonight show on 1 August, 1973,
> therefore, special precautions were taken and Geller
> was not permitted to get near enough to the table
> to jar it or touch the cans. He failed.[35]

As was stated before, much of what purports to be occultic
power is merely clever fraud. Geller is just one example of
many. However, there is also occult power which is genuinely
demonic, and some occult practitioners may even use a combination of demonic force and fraud. In fact, by Geller's own
admission, he may be in touch with what the Bible calls
demonic powers:

> They had taped what I had said. When they played

it back I was startled to hear my voice speaking in a distant and mechanical way. Under hypnosis, I apparently had put myself back in Cyprus: On the tape I was with my dog Joker. My voice said, as Andrija reports in his book: "I come here for learning. I just sit here in the dark with Joker. I learn and learn, but I don't know who is doing the teaching." Andrija's voice came on the tape to say: "What are you learning?" "It is about people who come from space. But I am not to talk about these things yet." "Is it secret?" Andrija's voice said on the tape. "Yes," my voice answered. "But someday you too will know."[36]

We must always remember that Satan is a deceiver and can use powers, normal or supernormal, to aid him in his deception of people.

Pantheism, Demonic Powers, and Prophecy

Christians readily admit that there are some truly paranormal powers. However, they deny that the source of these powers is divine. Instead, they attribute them to demonic power, examples of which are contained in the Bible. One "power" often hailed by pantheists as an example of psychic ability is the power to prophesy future events. Jeane Dixon is probably the best-known of the psychic prophets.

Occasionally some specific prophecies by modern seers and fortune-tellers come true. Sometimes this may be attributed to common sense ("Careful investments will secure your financial future"). Sometimes this may be attributed to coincidence or chance. Sometimes this may be attributed to demonic influence on actual events in the material world. But every single psychic prophet who occasionally scores right denies the cardinal doctrines of Christianity. The "fulfillment" of one or two of their prophecies is not used to glorify the Lord Jesus Christ, but to bring praise and power to the individual and/or occultic ends. Deuteronomy 13:1-3 declares that the prophet who prophesies correctly but leads a person to worship other gods is a liar and an enemy of God, and no one should follow him (or her).

However, by far the majority of the prophecies made by modern psychics don't come true. Deuteronomy 18:22 declares:

> When a prophet speaks in the name of the Lord,
> if the thing does not come about or come true, that
> is the thing which the Lord has not spoken. The
> prophet has spoken it presumptuously; you shall not
> be afraid of him.

Even Jeane Dixon's friend and biographer, Ruth Montgomery, admits that Dixon makes false prophecies, although she claims, in the face of overwhelming evidence to the contrary, that Dixon's failures are few: "Jean made a few forecasts that failed to occur. . . . She predicted that Red China would plunge the world into war over Quemoy and Matsu in October of 1958; she thought that labor leader Walter Reuther would actively seek the presidency in 1964."[37] According to the clear word of the Bible, a false prophecy is the mark of a false prophet.

There is also an occult connection between most of these modern false prophets and the world of demonism. Jeane Dixon, for example, uses a crystal ball, astrology, and telepathy, which are condemned by the Bible. Dixon's "call" to her role as prophet supposedly was given by a gypsy fortune-teller when she was a young girl.[38]

The Superiority of Biblical Divine Miracles

Moses performed miracles through the power of the one true and living God. This power was expressly for the purpose of convincing the Pharaoh of Egypt and his magicians that the Creator of the universe demanded freedom for his chosen people. The magicians of Egypt, although they were able to duplicate certain effects, could not master the miracles of the Most High God.

When Moses turned water into blood, the magicians followed suit (Exodus 7:19ff.). When Moses called for frogs by the word of the Lord, the magicians did also (Exodus 8:6ff.). But when God brought forth life from the dust, "the magicians tried with their secret arts to bring forth gnats, but they could not." They cried out, "This is the finger of God" (Exodus 8:18,19). The God of Moses proved himself superior to the gods of Egypt.

Similar "contests" between the living God and the false gods are recorded time and again in the Scriptures. Balak could not curse Israel because God intervened (Numbers 22—24). The prophets and gods of Baal were defeated by the God of Israel on Mount Carmel when Elijah called down fire from heaven to consume the sacrifice on the altar (1 Kings 18).

Even when there was a question or challenge from within Israel as to who rightly served as the spokesman of God, there was miraculous confirmation. Korah questioned Moses' divine authority and the earth swallowed him (Numbers 16). God vindicated Aaron by causing his rod to bud while the other 11 rods did not (Numbers 17). In the New Testament we find, "God [was] also bearing witness with them, both by signs and wonders and by various miracles and by gifts of the Holy Spirit according to His own will" (Hebrews 2:4).

Divine supernatural confirmation by the God of the Bible is superior to that of any of the supernormal events of the pantheistic, polytheistic, or occult religions.

The most dramatic differences between historic Christianity and all other religions comes in the supernatural divine ability to resurrect from the dead. This is not mere resuscitation, with the person later dying just as everyone must at one time, but true resurrection power, in which the resurrected person possesses a glorified and incorruptible body and never dies again. Jesus Christ, who was God manifest in the flesh, was killed and then resurrected from the dead through divine power, never to die again. His resurrection (which I will discuss in more detail in later chapters) is the ultimate testimony to the superiority of Christian theism over pantheistic naturalism. Jesus Christ said:

> No one has taken [my life] away from Me, but I lay it down on My own initiative. I have authority to lay it down, and I have authority to take it up again. This commandment I received from My Father (John 10:18).

CHAPTER 6

Atheism Attacks Christ

Christianity would be nothing without Jesus Christ. Christianity is more than just a code of morals. It is more than religious ideas. It is more than ritual and tradition. Christianity is centered and circumscribed by the person and work of Jesus Christ. To remove from Christianity the historical Jesus, the God-man who died for our sins, is to destroy Christianity. Christianity is a religion which claims exclusivity: It is not compatible with any other religion or world view. That exclusivity is based on Jesus Christ, who said, "I am the way, and the truth, and the life; no one comes to the Father but through Me" (John 14:6). Anyone who rejects Jesus Christ rejects God, Christianity, and eternal life. Christ declared, "My Father's will is that everyone who looks to the Son and believes in him shall have eternal life, and I will raise him up at the last day.... Everyone who listens to the Father and learns from him comes to me. No one has seen the Father except the one who is from God; only he has seen the Father. I tell you the truth, he who believes has everlasting life. I am the bread of life" (John 6:40,45-48 NIV).

Both atheism and pantheism attack the person and work of Jesus Christ. In this chapter we will examine the atheistic attacks on Jesus Christ, and in the next chapter we will examine the pantheistic attacks on Jesus Christ. We will answer these attacks, providing reasonable, historical, and evidential arguments for the person and work of Jesus Christ.

The Bible Tells Us Who Christ Is

At the center of Christianity stands Jesus Christ. Christians believe the Bible, which teaches us that Jesus Christ is eternally God, second Person of the Holy Trinity, who took on himself a new nature, a human nature, at his incarnation. We find three kinds of verses about Jesus Christ in the New Testament: those attesting to his deity, those attesting to his humanity, and those affirming that the one divine Person Jesus Christ has both a divine nature and a human nature.

Jesus Christ Is God

Jesus Christ is truly God. He testified of Himself:

> I and the Father are one (John 10:30).
> The Son of Man has authority on earth to forgive sins (Mark 2:10).
> Before Abraham was born, I am (John 8:58; cf. Isaiah 46:4).
> I am [the Christ]; and you shall see the Son of Man sitting at the right hand of Power, and coming with the clouds of heaven (Mark 14:62).
> He who does not honor the Son does not honor the Father who sent Him (John 5:23).
> I tell you that one greater than the temple is here. If you had known what these words mean, "I desire mercy, not sacrifice," you would not have condemned the innocent. For the Son of Man is Lord of the Sabbath (Matthew 12:6,7 NIV).
> Which is easier: to say to the paralytic, "Your sins are forgiven," or to say, "Get up, take your mat and walk"?

But that you may know that the Son of Man has authority on earth to forgive sins.... I tell you, get up, take your mat and go home (Mark 2:9-11 NIV).

Behold, I am coming soon! My reward is with me, and I will give to everyone according to what he has done. I am the Alpha and the Omega, the First and the Last, the Beginning and the End (Revelation 22:12,13 NIV).

In addition to Christ's own words, there are numerous declarations in Scripture which affirm the deity of Christ. The following are a few examples:

In the beginning was the Word, and the Word was with God, and the Word was God.... The Word became flesh and lived for a while among us. We have seen his glory, the glory of the one and only Son, who came from the Father, full of grace and truth (John 1:1,14 NIV).

...he was even calling God his own Father, making himself equal with God (John 5:18 NIV).

Thomas said to [Jesus], "My Lord and my God!" (John 20:28 NIV).

Theirs are the patriarchs, and from them is traced the human ancestry of Christ, who is God over all, forever praised! (Romans 9:5 NIV).

He is the image of the invisible God, the firstborn over all creation. For by him all things were created: things in heaven and on earth, visible and invisible, whether thrones or power or rulers or authorities; all things were created by him and for him. He is before all things, and in him all things hold together (Colossians 1:15-17 NIV).

For in Christ all the fullness of the Deity lives in bodily form (Colossians 2:9 NIV).

We wait for the blessed hope—the glorious appearing of our great God and Savior, Jesus Christ (Titus 2:13 NIV).

About the Son he says, "Your throne, O God, will last for ever and ever, and righteousness will be the scepter of your kingdom" (Hebrews 1:8 NIV).

To those who through the righteousness of our God and Savior Jesus Christ have received a faith as precious as ours (2 Peter 1:1 NIV).

The Church Acknowledges Christ's Deity

The orthodox Christian church has always upheld the deity of Jesus Christ. From the apostles onward, through the persecuted church of the early centuries, through the Middle Ages, through the Reformation, and to the present, the church has always upheld the deity of Christ. The earliest statements of faith used by the church to summarize biblical teaching (called creeds) centered on the person and work of Jesus Christ.

The Nicene Creed was formulated after resolution of the Arian controversy in the fourth century. Arius of Alexandria taught that Jesus Christ was created by the Father and was not the eternal true God. Orthodoxy won out against Arius and his followers, summarizing the biblical view of Christ this way:

> We believe in one God the Father Almighty, Maker of heaven and earth, of all things visible and invisible; and in one Lord Jesus Christ, the only-begotten Son of God, begotten from the Father before all time, Light of Light, true God of true God, begotten, not created, consubstantial with the Father, through Whom all things came into being. . . .

Remember, the church did not "invent" Jesus Christ or "mythologize" him from some unimportant rural Jewish teacher. The church has submitted itself to Jesus Christ as Lord and Savior because he is God and revealed himself to be God, proving his claims by his resurrection from the dead—not because people imagined him to be God. The Chalcedon Creed (451) succinctly summarized what the Bible taught about the person of Jesus Christ:

...our Lord Jesus Christ, at once complete in Godhead and complete in manhood, truly God and truly
man, consisting also of a reasonable soul and body;
of one substance with the Father as regards his
Godhead, and at the same time of one substance with
us as regards his manhood; like us in all respects
apart from sin.

Atheists Attack the Person and Work of Jesus Christ

Atheists reject the biblical orthodox doctrines of the person and work of Jesus Christ. Since atheists reject belief in
any idea of God, they must reject belief in anything supernatural. Since they reject God and the supernatural, they must
also reject the person and work of Jesus Christ. First, many
atheists reject the idea that Jesus Christ even existed, much
less that he could have been God. Second, many atheists reject
the deity and resurrection of Christ by maintaining that Jesus
did not really die on the cross, but was an ordinary man who
escaped death on the cross through one or more schemes.
(These atheists would, of course, maintain that he died like
any other man at some later time.) Third, many atheists assert
that Jesus Christ did die on the cross, but never rose again,
giving one or more explanations to substantiate their position.
Fourth, many atheists assume that Jesus Christ was not God
and did not rise from death, and then on that assumption build
an attack on Christ's character. We will review each of these
four atheistic attacks below and then provide reasonable and
biblical responses to each of them.

Jesus Christ Never Existed

All atheists deny that Jesus is God, but some even doubt
that Jesus Christ ever lived. This view seems hard to believe,
given the wealth of eyewitness testimony presented in the historical records of the New Testament. However, the atheists who

doubt the existence of Jesus Christ do so by rejecting outright anything from the New Testament. To them the New Testament is completely without value as evidence or history concerning Jesus Christ. Once they have dismissed the New Testament documents, they are then free to dismiss the existence of Christ altogether.

The British mathematician and agnostic Bertrand Russell, who wrote a popular defense of his agnosticism called *Why I Am Not a Christian*, argued that "historically it is quite doubtful whether Christ ever existed at all, and if he did we do not know anything about him...."[1]

The famous liberal missionary Albert Schweitzer said, "The Jesus of Nazareth who came forward publicly as the Messiah, who preached the ethic of the Kingdom of God...and died to give his work its final consecration, never had any existence."[2]

The American founding father Thomas Paine is a good representative of those atheists who reject the New Testament and then claim they can know nothing of Jesus Christ from "history." He said, "There is no history written at the time Jesus Christ is said to have lived that speaks of the existence of such a person, even as a man."[3]

Jesus' Death and Resurrection Are Myth

How do atheists who deny Jesus' existence explain the New Testament "story"? They claim that the New Testament story is patterned after ancient myths and is itself a myth. While most of us think of myths as made-up adventure fantasies, sort of like Superman comics today, myths are considered to be serious literary forms. In the literary sense, a *myth* is a story which contains supernatural elements and/or figures and is used by a primitive people to explain or describe in types a primitive world view. It is not just idle children's entertainment: It is a serious, though inaccurate, attempt by primitive people to understand their world.

This is what many atheists claim for the New Testament.

This view was popularized by the famous nineteenth-century mythologist, James Frazer, in his now-classic *The Golden Bough* (1890). It is a view still espoused by some atheists, including John H. Randall, emeritus professor of philosophy at Columbia University, who asserted, "Christianity, at the hands of Paul, became a mystical system of redemption, much like the cult of Isis, and the other sacramental or mystery religions of the day."[4]

A more popular supporter of this view is Hugh J. Schonfield, whose books about the myths of the New Testament and Jesus Christ have been bestsellers for years, and whose *Passover Plot* was made into a major motion picture several years ago. Schonfield noted, "The revelations of Frazer in *The Golden Bough* had not got through to the masses.... Christians remained related under the skin to the devotees of Adonis and Osiris, Dionysus and Mithras."[5]

Jesus Christ Did Not Die on the Cross

Some atheists believe that Jesus Christ may have been a historical figure, and may even have been crucified, but they deny that he died on the cross. Instead, they postulate, he survived his crucifixion and died later like any other man.

This theory did not originate with liberal atheistic scholars of the last two centuries. On the contrary, it is a theory at least 1300 years old. This is the theory that Mohammed broached in the *Quran*, the book of revelations held sacred by Muslims. The *Quran* asserts concerning Jesus Christ:

> But they killed him not,
> Nor crucified him,
> But so it was made
> To appear to them,
> And those who differ
> Therein are full of doubts,
> With no [certain] knowledge,

But only conjecture to follow,
For of a surety
They killed him not....[6]

   Although Islam is a religion, and Muslims are not atheistic, some Muslim arguments against the death on the cross and
resurrection of Christ are the same as arguments used by
atheists. Islam is the fastest growing world religion today, and
Muslim spokesmen are promoting Islam aggressively, usually
by arguing against Christianity. One popular Muslim apologist
is Ahmed Deedat, who debated Christian apologist Josh
McDowell.* In that debate Deedat listed 12 major reasons why
he did not believe that Jesus Christ had died on the cross. Those
reasons are summarized here:

   1. Jesus claimed that he had not a spiritualized resurrection body (Luke 24:36).
   2. Mary went to the tomb to "anoint" (massage)
Jesus (John 20:1), which is only done to live bodies.
   3. Only a live human body, not a resurrected spiritual
body, would need the stone rolled away from the tomb
and the burial cloth removed.
   4. Jesus disguised himself as a gardener out of fear
that the Jews would try again to kill him when they found
out they failed the first time.
   5. Mary came to the tomb to take Jesus away to rest
(recuperate), something of which a dead corpse would
be incapable.
   6. Jesus refused to let Mary embrace him because he
was still in pain from his wounds.
   7. Jesus said his resurrection would be like Jonah's
(Matthew 12:38-40). Jonah did not die in the fish's belly;
he was only trapped for three days.

---

* The debate is contained in *The Islam Debate*, by Josh McDowell
and John Gilchrist (San Bernardino, CA: Here's Life Publishers,
1983).

8. There is not claim by Christ in the entire New Testament that "I was dead and now I have come back from the dead."

9. Jesus did not plan to die, as is evidenced by the fact that he took disciples and swords with him to the garden for defense.

10. Jesus prayed in the garden to be delivered from death, and God sent an angel to help him.

11. Even Pilate marveled when he heard that Jesus had died after only three hours on the cross. In reality, he fainted.

12. Jesus' bones were not broken on the cross, as was the custom with those who had died.

These 12 reasons constitute most of the religious and nonreligious arguments against the death and resurrection of Jesus Christ. Atheists would not accept all 12 reasons. For example, reason ten assumes the existence of God and the validity of miracles. However, atheists can and have used most of these arguments in their fights against Christianity.

The similarities in their arguments are illustrated by atheist writer B. C. Johnson in his *Atheist Debators' Handbook*. He argues in a circle for his point, assuming the impossibility of resurrection before he argues that "the very fact that a supposedly dead man was seen alive after his reported death is an indication that he was never dead in the first place." Furthermore, he says:

> Crucifixion was a slow death. Pilate expressed urprise that Jesus was dead so soon (Mark 15:44). Jesus was taken down from the cross much sooner than he would otherwise have been, because it was the beginning of the Sabbath, during which no crucifixion was permitted (John 19:31).[7]

Johnson's assertions show us the close parallels between Muslim and atheistic arguments against the death of Jesus Christ on the cross.

Jesus Did Not Rise from the Dead

Other atheists agree that Jesus Christ died on the cross but deny that he rose from the dead. They cannot admit any miracle, or supernatural event, since they do not accept the existence of anything outside the natural world, such as God. The atheist argument against Christ's resurrection takes various forms.

In order to account for the empty tomb three days after the crucifixion, some argue that the body must have been stolen by Jesus' disciples to make it *look* like he rose from the dead. This argument is even older than the Muslim arguments. It is recorded in the New Testament (Matthew 28:11-15):

> While the women were on their way, some of the guards went into the city and reported to the chief priests everything that had happened. When the chief priests had met with the elders and devised a plan, they gave the soldiers a large sum of money, telling them, "You are to say, 'His disciples came during the night and stole him away while we were asleep.' If this report gets to the governor, we will satisfy him and keep you out of trouble." So the soldiers took the money and did as they were instructed. And this story has been widely circulated among the Jews to this very day (NIV).

This theory was revived by the eighteenth-century deist H. S. Reimarus. He believed that Jesus' disciples stole his body and announced that he was a spiritual king with a future kingdom.

A number of atheists misinterpret the resurrection account passage in Matthew 28:1-8 concerning the women's trip to the empty tomb. They declare that the reason the tomb was empty was that the women accidentally went to the wrong tomb! Their confusion was caused by the bad light at early dawn and by their tear-filled eyes, which clouded their vision.

According to liberal theologian Kirsopp Lake, the women went to the wrong tomb at dawn on the first day of the week. The caretaker was there, and he told them, "You are looking for Jesus of Nazareth. He is not here." The caretaker meant that he was not at that tomb, but at a different one in the garden. The flustered women fled with this story, and when the disciples later had visions of Christ, they reinterpreted this story into the angelic announcement of the resurrection of Christ.[8]

The view above is similar to the hallucination view. Lake decided that the women went to the wrong tomb and then the disciples had "visions" of Christ. The hallucination view holds that the entire resurrection tradition is based on hallucinations. The disciples never saw Jesus alive after his crucifixion. Their experience was purely subjective. There was no objective basis in reality for the dreams, visions, or experiences of seeing Jesus after his crucifixion.

David Strauss popularized this view in 1835, suggesting that the pure air of Galilee produced hallucinatory "memories" of Jesus' teachings among some of his disciples after his death. Many nineteenth-century critics applied this view to the so-called "resurrection appearances" of Christ and concluded that there was no basis in fact—only in fantasy—for the resurrection of Christ.

Some atheists who agree that Jesus really did die on the cross explain the resurrection appearances by claiming that the disciples mistook other people for Jesus. *Passover Plot* author Hugh Schonfield supports this view, criticizing those who hold the hallucination view:

> We are not dealing in the Gospels with hallucinations, with psychic phenomena or survival in the Spiritualist sense. These possibilities do not fit the circumstances as they are narrated. However the traditions of the resurrection of Jesus are to be explained, it cannot legitimately be on these lines.[9]

Such atheists argue, for example, that Mary Magdalene mistook the gardener for Jesus. The two disciples mistook a stranger to be Jesus. Jesus did not rise from the dead. He was not the Son of God. He was only a mortal man who died like any other man and never rose again.

Jesus' Character Is Flawed

Often atheists will acknowledge that Jesus Christ existed, and that he was crucified. However, they will deny his resurrection and deny that he was the Son of God. Their best estimations of Christ's character fall far short of the New Testament picture of his character.

Friedrich Nietzsche, whose virulent attacks on Christianity and belief in God fueled much of the modern atheistic movement, mocked the idea that Jesus was intelligent, or a genius, saying, "An entirely different word would still be more fitting here—the word *idiot*."[10]

Agnostic Bertrand Russell criticized Christ's morals, stating, "There is one very serious defect to my mind in Christ's moral character, and that is that he believed in hell."[11] Russell also criticized Jesus' attitude toward animals, citing his casting of the demons into the pigs who then drowned themselves as an indication of his cruelty. Russell mocked the biblical claim for Jesus' wisdom and knowledge, since Christ predicted he would return immediately after his ascension, but still hasn't after nearly 2000 years. Russell concluded that there were many historical figures whose characters he admired more than that of Jesus:

> I cannot myself feel that either in the matter of wisdom or in the matter of virtue Christ stands quite as high as some other people known to history. I think I should put Buddha and Socrates above him in those respects.[12]

Not all atheists are as critical of Christ's character. Although they will not accord him the deity and sinlessness attributed to him by Scripture, they will acknowledge him as a sincere man—deluded or fraudulent, but sincere. The *Passover Plot* summarizes this view of Christ's character:

> He was no charlatan, willfully and deliberately misleading his people, well knowing that his posing as the Messiah was fraudulent. There is not the slightest suspicion of pretense on his part. On the contrary, no one could be more sure of his vocation than was Jesus, and not even the threat of imminent death by the horrible torture of crucifixion could make him deny his messiahship.[13]

Schonfield concludes that "the historical Jesus has always been there for the finding, not faultless, not inerrant, not divine, but magnificently human."[14]

The attacks against the deity and person of Jesus Christ by atheists are part of the atheistic world view and must be answered by Scripture, evidence, and sound reasoning. Let us now respond to the above objections with Christian answers.

A Christian Response to Atheistic Attacks

This Christian response to atheistic attacks on Jesus Christ presents ten major focuses:

1. The existence of God.
2. Christian theism.
3. The New Testament.
4. Jesus Christ is not mythological.
5. Jesus Christ really died on the cross.
6. Jesus Christ's body was not stolen.
7. The disciples did not go to the wrong tomb.
8. Christ's followers did not hallucinate his resurrection.
9. Other people were not mistaken for Jesus Christ.

10. Christ's character is consistent with his deity
    and resurrection.

The Existence of God

Atheists must argue against the deity, person, and resurrection of Jesus Christ because they must uphold their antitheistic assumptions. If there is no God, then of course Jesus Christ could not be God. However, if God exists, then it is logically possible that Jesus Christ could be that God.

Rejecting the existence of God is the "article of faith" which most prevents atheists from believing in the deity, person, and resurrection of Jesus Christ. As the preceding chapters have shown, however, the atheistic assumption is not correct. The most reasonable view, taking into account reasoning and external evidence (science, history, etc.), is that a supreme, eternal, necessary Being outside this universe created this universe. This Being is God. The informed atheist must abandon reason and science to maintain his allegiance to atheism. Establishing the existence of God removes the largest barrier between atheism and the deity of Christ.

Christian Theism

Once one has established that God the Creator exists, one must establish Christian theism. Even if the atheist is convinced that God created the universe, he still may argue that this God would not or could not interfere in his creation, and thus could not incarnate as Jesus Christ or any other individual. This was also covered in earlier chapters, where it was established that all other alternate views of God are unreasonable and/or contrary to evidence.

So, given that God exists, and that God has the ability and desire to interact with his creation, the remaining objections to the deity and person of Christ can be answered systematically below.

The New Testament

The New Testament is the most complete and reliable ancient document we have attesting to the nature and person of Jesus Christ. All discussion of Jesus Christ is determined by one's view of Scripture. Atheism attacks the reliability and inspiration of Scripture as a foundation to its various arguments against the resurrection of Jesus Christ. The following is a summary of the most relevant evidence and argumentation establishing the truthworthiness of the New Testament.

Out of all ancient literature, the New Testament is the most well-authenticated document. There are more manuscripts of the New Testament, plus earlier and more reliable copies of the original manuscripts (autographs) of the New Testament, than of any other written work from ancient times.

Some copies of portions of the New Testament can be dated at as little as 100 years from the date the autographs were composed. Through the science of textual criticism, even the more numerous later copies provide invaluable aid in determining what the original texts said. The chart on the following page summarizes the comparative evidence showing the superiority of the manuscript evidence for the New Testament.

There are several significant points to note from this chart. First of all, the New Testament (in parts and whole) survives in over 5300 hand-copied manuscripts (up until its first mechanical printing), while most other classical works survive in fewer than two dozen. Even with so few copies, scholars are able to trust, through the application of textual criticism, that the copies we possess of such works are accurate representations of the originals. How much more can we trust that the text we possess of the New Testament is an accurate representation of what was written originally!

Second, the time gap between the date of composition and our earliest copies (or partial copies) of classical works is usually around 1000 years. It is remarkable that those copies have preserved the purity of the original text. And yet the purity of the New Testament text is even better safeguarded, since our

MANUSCRIPT EVIDENCE FOR SOME CLASSICAL TEXTS

Author/Text	Date Written	Earliest Copies	Time Gap (Yrs.)	# Copies
Herodotus/History	400 B.C.	900 A.D.	1300	8
Thucydides/History	400 B.C.	900 A.D.	1300	8
Plato	400 B.C.	900 A.D.	1300	7
Demosthenes	300 B.C.	1100 A.D.	1400	200
Aristotle	300 B.C.	1100 A.D.	1400	5
Caesar/Gallic Wars	100 B.C.	900 A.D.	900	10
Livy/Roman History	30 A.D.	900 A.D.	900	20
Tacitus/Annals	100 A.D.	1100 A.D.	1000	20
Pliny/History	100 A.D.	900 A.D.	800	7
New Testament	100 A.D.	200 A.D.	100	5300

earliest copies of Greek texts of the majority of the New Testament are a mere 100 years from the furthest dates for New Testament composition. No other text from the ancient world is nearly as reliable as the New Testament text.

In addition to this early Greek manuscript testimony to the New Testament, we find almost all of the New Testament (minus 11 verses) preserved as quotations in the writings of the early church leaders who lived during the first 400 years of church history. (See the chart on the following page.)

In addition to the overwhelming evidence for the reliability of the text of the New Testament, there is abundant evidence that the New Testament books were written soon after the events they reported, by contemporaries of Jesus Christ.

Before modern archaeological studies, some scholars decided that the life and teachings of the real Jesus Christ were lost in the obscurity of the early church. The Jesus Christ presented in the New Testament, they reasoned, was largely the manufacture (mythologizing) of the second- or third-century church, which had a religious need to deify Christ and attribute to this simple Jewish teacher miracles and profound teachings.

Extensive archaeological and historical research, in addition to refinements in literary (higher) criticism, have forced objective scholars to acknowledge the early composition of the New Testament. (There are still popular writers who repeat the destructive higher criticism of the nineteenth century, such as Ian Wilson in *Jesus: The Evidence*, but their lack of scholarship is evident to anyone who knows the field.) Objective scholars, even if they do not believe what the New Testament records teach, acknowledge that the basic books of the New Testament were written within the lifetime of Jesus' apostles.

The noted Anglican bishop John A. T. Robinson (author of the liberal *Honest to God*) reevaluated the dates of the New Testament composition and concluded in his *Redating the New Testament* (summarized in his popular *Can We Trust the New Testament?*) that the majority of the New Testament was composed before 70 A.D. This places the written core of the New

THE CHURCH FATHERS QUOTE VERSES OF
THE NEW TESTAMENT

Writer	Gospels	Acts	Letters of Paul	General Letters	Revelation	Totals
Justin Martyr	268	10	43	6	3	330
Irenaeus	1038	194	499	23	65	1819
Clement of Alex.	1017	44	1127	207	11	2406
Origen	9231	349	7778	399	165	17922
Tertullian	3822	502	2609	120	205	7258
Hippolytus	734	42	387	27	188	1378
Eusebius	3258	211	1592	88	27	5176
TOTALS	19368	1352	14035	870	664	36289

Testament at only ten to 15 years after Jesus' death and resurrection:

Book	Date of Composition
1 Corinthians	Spring, 55 A.D.
Mark	c. 45-60 A.D.
Matthew	c. 40-60 A.D.
Luke	c. 57-60 A.D.
Jude	61-62 A.D.
Acts	57-62 A.D.
John	c. 40-65 A.D.[15]

Liberal New Testament scholar and form critic C. H. Dodd, while not embracing Robinson's views wholeheartedly, admitted:

> You are certainly justified in questioning the whole structure of the accepted "critical" chronology of the New Testament writings, which avoids putting anything earlier than 70, so that none of them are available for anything like first-generation testimony. I should agree with you that much of this late dating is quite arbitrary, even wanton, the offspring not of any argument that can be presented, but rather of the position of the critic's prejudice that if he appears to assent to the traditional position of the early church he will be thought no better than a stick-in-the-mud.[16]

Other world-acclaimed scholars have come to recognize, based on the evidence, the early dates for the writing of the New Testament. Few archaeologists ever enjoyed greater acclaim than the renowned William F. Albright, who said, based on his decades of archaeological research, "In my opinion, every book of the New Testament was written by a baptized Jew between the forties and the eighties of the first century A.D. (very probably between about 50 and 75 A.D.)"[17] New Testament archaeologist Nelson Glueck states, "We can already say emphatically that there is no longer any solid basis for dating any book of the New Testament after about A.D. 80.''[18]

In summary, the New Testament Gospels were written during the lives of the contemporaries of Christ. Hence, they do not allow for the time necessary for mythologizing to take place. We can safely trust that the text we possess in our common translations today is an accurate representation of what Christ's contemporaries actually wrote.

Many early archaeologists of the last century began their research in the lands of the New Testament with little confidence that they could trust the New Testament documents to give them information useful in their research. They were often steeped in destructive higher criticism, and assumed that the New Testament records were historically unreliable. However, as archaeology became more and more sophisticated, and archaeology of the biblical lands especially progressed, these assumptions were challenged by the evidence.

Archaeologist Sir William Ramsey did more in his career to substantiate the records of Luke and Acts than has any archaeologist before or since. However, he did not begin by thinking he could support the New Testament record. The evidence changed his mind:

> I began with a mind unfavorable to [Acts], for the ingenuity and apparent completeness of the Tubingen theory [destructive higher criticism] had at one time quite convinced me. It did not lie then in my line of life to investigate the subject minutely; but more recently I found myself often brought in contact with the book of Acts as an authority for the topography, antiquities, and society of Asia Minor. It was gradually borne in upon me that in various details the narrative showed marvelous truth.[19]

What Ramsey discovered over the course of his career was

that Luke, the author of the Gospel and the book of Acts, was a first-rate historian who, in making reference to 32 countries, 54 cities, and nine islands, made *no* historical errors!

Biblical archaeologist Millar Burrows affirmed, "Archaeological work has unquestionably strengthened confidence in the reliability of the scriptural record. More than one archaeologist has found his respect for the Bible increased by the experience of excavation in Palestine."[20]

Archaeologist Nelson Glueck made the following claim, amply supported by the evidence:

> As a matter of fact, however, it may be stated categorically that no archaeological discovery has ever controverted a biblical reference. Scores of archaeological findings have been made which confirm in clear outline or exact detail historical statements in the Bible.[21]

In summary, both in detail and in broad statement, the New Testament documents have been confirmed overwhelmingly by modern archaeological evidence. We can trust that the New Testament documents are archaeologically truthful.

In the vast scope of Roman world history of the first century, Jesus Christ was an obscure preacher from a rural area of an insignificant corner of the Roman Empire. There was no reason for the historical documents of the time (excluding the primary New Testament documents) to mention him at all. And yet we do have some acknowledgment of Jesus Christ from secular historians of the first and early second centuries.

The Roman historian Tacitus (A.D. 112) wrote of Christ (*Christus*) as follows:

> Christus, the founder of the name, was put to death by Pontius Pilate, procurator of Judea in the reign of Tiberius: but the pernicious superstition, repressed for a time, broke out again, not only through Judea, where the mischief originated, but through the city of Rome also.[22]

The Jewish historian Flavius Josephus was even closer in time and location to the events than Tacitus, and he made reference to Jesus in these words:

> At this time there was a wise man who was called Jesus. And his conduct was good, and [he] was known to be virtuous. And many people from among the Jews and the other nations became his disciples. Pilate condemned him to be crucified and to die. And those who had become his disciples did not abandon his discipleship. They reported that he had appeared to them three days after his crucifixion and that he was alive; accordingly, he was perhaps the Messiah concerning whom the prophets have recounted wonders.[23]

In the second century the Roman historian Seutonius recounted another historian's note concerning Christ, saying, "Another Roman historian, court official under Hadrian, annalist of the Imperiod House, says: 'As the Jews were making constant disturbances at the instigation of Chrestus [alternate spelling of Christus], he expelled them from Rome.' "[24] The other historian evidently thought that Christ was personally leading the Jewish Christians in Rome, and so laid the blame for the Jewish expulsion from Rome (in A.D. 49) on Christ.

The Roman governor of Bithyma in Asia Minor, Pliny the Younger, wrote this to the Emperor concerning Christians in A.D. 112:

> They affirmed, however, that the whole of their guilt, or their error, was, that they were in the habit of meeting on a certain fixed day before it was light, when they sang in alternate verse a hymn to Christ as to a god, and bound themselves to a solemn oath, not to any wicked deeds, but never to commit any fraud, theft, adultery, never to falsify their word,

not to deny a trust when they should be called upon
to deliver it up.[25]

In addition to ancient secular writers mentioning Christ, the
ancient Jewish Talmud also mentions him, although not
flatteringly, saying:

> On the eve of Passover they hanged Yeshu [of
> Nazareth] and the herald went before him for forty
> days saying [Yeshu of Nazareth] is going forth to
> be stoned in that he hath practiced sorcery and
> beguiled and led astray Israel. Let everyone know-
> ing aught in his defense come and plead for him.
> But they found naught in his defense and hanged
> him on the eve of Passover.[26]

The early Christian apologist and writer Justin Martyr (A.D.
150) referred to an imperial record of the life, death, and
miracles of Christ in these words, "And that He did those
things, you can learn from the Acts of Pontius Pilate."[27]

We can summarize this section by affirming that the New
Testament record has been attested to by secular history close
to the time of its writing.

Modern historians who concentrate their historical studies
in the period and area of the New Testament events have seen,
on the basis of the historical evidence, the remarkable historicity of the New Testament record.

A. N. Sherwin-White is an eminent historian of Roman times
contemporary to the life of Christ. He chides critical theologians for not recognizing that the New Testament is a
valuable historical document, especially when it is compared
with Roman sources. He points out that Roman history is based
on documents which are at least one or two generations
(sometimes one or two centuries) removed from the events.
Yet historians rely on these late records to reconstruct the events
of the Roman world.[28] The New Testament is even more trust-
worthy, having been written by contemporaries of the events.

In summary, the New Testament is accurate and reliable. It is the best-attested history and biography we have of any classical period, event, or person. Atheists try to reject the deity and resurrection of Jesus Christ by rejecting the documents which attest to them. However, as we have seen, to reject the historicity of the New Testament is unreasonable. If one is consistent, then he must also reject all other classical history, which is less well-documented than is the New Testament. The only way one can preserve the rest of classical history and still reject the historicity of the New Testament is to be inconsistent, the very trait of which atheists falsely accuse Christians!

Jesus Christ Is Not Mythological

Our fourth response to the atheistic attack on Jesus Christ is to answer the challenge that the Gospel record of Jesus Christ is a myth, a legend, a made-up story developed by the early church in response to emotional needs.

Professor Sherwin-White, quoted above, mentions one strong argument against the mythologizing of Jesus Christ: There was not enough time between the historical figure and the historical documents for a myth or legend to develop.[29] This is echoed by legend expert Julius Muller:

> One cannot imagine how such a series of legends could arise in an historical age, obtain universal respect, and supplant the historical recollection of the true character and connexion of their heroes' lives in the minds of the community, if eyewitnesses were still at hand, who could be questioned respecting the truth of the recorded marvels.[30]

In other words, legends don't develop as long as the eyewitnesses are alive. It usually takes two generations or more for a legend to develop. (It should not be surprising, then, that the apocryphal gospels were composed during the second and third centuries.) The New Testament, on the other hand, is literature of the contemporaries of Jesus Christ, and has all the signs of authentic history.

Even skeptical historians have acknowledged the marks of authenticity and the lack of myth characteristics in the New Testament. Popular historian Will Durant said of the Gospel writers:

> They record many incidents that mere inventors would have concealed—the competition of the apostles for high places in the kingdom, their flight after Jesus' arrest, Peter's denial, the failure of Christ to work miracles in Galilee, the references of some auditors to his possible insanity.... No one reading these scenes can doubt the reality of the figure behind them.[31]

The myth view of Jesus Christ mentioned in the first part of this chapter fails to recognize the significant difference between nonchristian belief in a spiritual afterlife (immortality) and Christian belief in the bodily resurrection. As the noted Dead Sea Scroll scholar John Pryke observed, "The bliss of the elect as described in the Manual [of the Dead Sea Essene sect] is much nearer to the 'immortality of the soul' than to the 'resurrection of the flesh.' "[32]

The myth view also fails to account for the important difference between nonchristian belief in reincarnation (into a different body) and Christian belief in resurrection (of the same body). The myth view fails to understand that the Old Testament, not Greek and Roman mythology, is the source of New Testament teaching. Far from borrowing from pagan sources, the New Testament writers were scrupulous in their adherence to the truths revealed in the Old Testament, and continually contrasted the gospel message with pagan mythology (see, for example, Acts 28:1-6 and 2 Peter 1:16).

The idea that the Jesus Christ of our New Testament is the product of myth-making by the second- and third-century church ignores the open vows of the New Testament writers

that they are eyewitnesses and that they are telling the truth.
For example, 1 John 1:1,2 says, "That which was from the
beginning, which we have heard, which we have seen with our
eyes, which we have looked at and our hands have touched—
this we proclaim concerning the Word of life. The life
appeared; we have seen it and testify to it, and we proclaim
to you the eternal life, which was with the Father and has
appeared to us" (NIV). Not only did the writers claim to be
eyewitnesses, but they also claimed to be preserving right teaching (orthodoxy) in the face of heresy. They fought vigorously
against mythologizing (see, for example, John 21:22-25).

To claim that the New Testament portrayal of Jesus Christ
is a myth of later origin is to ignore the objective historical,
textual, and reasonable evidence.

Jesus Christ Really Died on the Cross

In response to the critics' charges that Christ never really
died on the cross, let us look at the evidence, especially that
from the primary source documents, the New Testament
Gospels.

The apparent-death theory fails to recognize the fatal extent
of Jesus' injuries. Jesus had not slept the night before his
crucifixion. He was beaten several times and flogged before
the crucifixion. He was so weak that he collapsed while carry-
ing his cross, and had to be helped by a bystander. (Even if
he only had to carry the crosspiece, that heavy timber was
enough to overcome him.) Jesus' hands and feet were nailed
to the cross, meaning that he bled for an extended period
(perhaps as long as seven hours—see Mark 15:25,33,42).
Crucifixion itself induces the lungs to collapse, leading to
suffocation. (That is why the custom was to break the legs of
the crucified, so that he would be unable to raise himself high
enough for his weakened lungs to ventilate.) Finally, Jesus'
side was pierced by a spear and "blood and water" came forth,
an indication of the pooling of the blood in death.

The apparent-death view also fails to account for the

circumstances of Christ's death and burial. As just mentioned, the "blood and water" which gushed from Christ's side when it was pierced is conclusive evidence of death. The famous Dublin physiologist Samuel Houghton, M.D., said, "There remains, therefore, no supposition possible to explain the recorded phenomenon except the combination of the crucifixion and rupture of the heart."[33] Dr. Houghton's conclusion echoed that of Dr. William Stroud, who had earlier authored the definitive *The Physiological Cause of the Death of Christ* (1847). Dr. Houghton wrote, "That rupture of the heart was the cause of the death of Christ is ably maintained by Dr. William Stroud; and that rupture of the heart actually occurred I firmly believe...."[34] If this is what happened to Christ, then he was already dead when the spear pierced him. (If he were not already dead, surely the great and traumatic loss of blood at that time would have killed him almost immediately.) The Romans were so convinced that Jesus was already dead that they did not break his legs (see above), a customary "humanitarian" gesture to hasten the crucified's death:

> But when they came to Jesus and found that he was already dead, they did not break his legs. Instead, one of the soldiers pierced Jesus' side with a spear, bringing a sudden flow of blood and water. The man who saw it has given testimony, and his testimony is true. He knows that he tells the truth, and he testifies so that you also may believe (John 19:33-35 NIV).

Taking no chances, Pilate even checked with the centurion to make sure that Jesus was really dead before he surrendered his body to Joseph of Arimathea:

> Pilate was surprised to hear that he was already dead. Summoning the centurion, he asked him if Jesus had already died. When he learned from the centurion that it was so, he gave the body to Joseph (Mark 15:44,45 NIV).

Joseph and Nicodemus took the body of Jesus and wrapped it in approximately 100 pounds of spices and burial cloth (John 19:39) and then laid it in a sealed tomb, in front of which Pilate had posted guards. Far from being drugged and revived in the "coolness of the tomb," this fact plus the fact that Jesus specifically refused to take the drug-soaked sponge offered him at the beginning of his crucifixion (Matthew 27:34) combine to show that Jesus must have been dead, not drugged, in the tomb.

All of the evidence from the primary-source historical documents (the Gospels themselves) supports the fact that Jesus Christ actually died on the cross. Any atheistic attempt to deny that fact must also deny all of the evidence.

Jesus Christ's Body Was Not Stolen

There are many reasonable and evidential answers to the "stolen-body" hypothesis often posed by atheists. Six reasons will suffice for our review here.

One, there was no motive for robbers stealing the body. There was nothing of recoverable value in the tomb. The soldiers had cast lots for his robe; the graveclothes were left behind. There is no value in a dead corpse.

Two, the tomb was sealed and guarded. Robbers could never have succeeded in their plot.

Three, the assumption of the texts is that only Joseph and the women knew where the body was buried (the disciples having fled in sorrow and shame).

Four, it is unthinkable that any of the disciples stole the body. It would have been opposed to the very teachings of the man they had claimed as their master. It would have been opposed to their own moral characters, as attested to by their lives, teachings, and willingness to die for their beliefs. It is also likely that, had they tried such an idea, they would have been caught at the tomb by the guards there. Finally, according to the primary documents, the disciples themselves were reluctant to believe in the resurrection until they had seen the resurrected Christ for themselves. If they had plotted to steal his body to fake a resurrection, they would have been the first to champion such a story.

Five, it is irrational to hypothesize that devout disciples, even ones unscrupulous enough to steal the body, would carefully unwrap that body, leave the graveclothes, and sneak off with the naked corpse!

Six, the stolen-body hypothesis ignores the postresurrection appearances of the risen Christ. Who was this *live* body that kept appearing for 40 days to over 500 people, including all 11 of the original disciples? (Judas was dead.) All the people he appeared to had known him before his death, and were not likely to be fooled by a warmed-over corpse or a clever impostor.

It is fanciful speculation and mythologizing to declare that the body of Christ was stolen from the tomb.

No One Mistook Christ's Tomb

That few skeptics hold the view that the tomb was misidentified is understandable, given the historical record. It lacks any credibility.

Pilate knew where the tomb was: He ordered a guard posted there. The Jewish leaders knew where the tomb was: They conspired after the resurrection with the tomb guards. Joseph of Arimathea knew where the tomb was: It was his tomb. No one can reasonably assert that the location of Christ's tomb was lost and that this led to the "resurrection myth."

The Disciples Were Not Hallucinating the Resurrection

The hallucination view, like the others, is a denial of the credibility of the Gospel accounts, which we have shown to be reliable historical records. It does not account for the miraculous transformation of the disciples and for the growth of early Christianity, which was based not on fanciful religious stories but on the testable facts of the death, burial, and resurrection of Jesus Christ. The apostle Paul declared that the heart of the Gospel was the death, burial and resurrection of Jesus Christ (1 Corinthians 15:1-4), and he challenged nonbelievers of his day to disprove these facts (see Acts 26:26).

Those who are skeptical of an experience do not hallucinate that experience. Hallucination results when a person wants to believe that something is true and so "sees" it as true even though it isn't. The disciples, on the other hand, did not believe the resurrection and had given up their faith until they were confronted with the resurrected Christ.

The hallucination view does not account for the large number of people (500) on numerous occasions (ten) who saw the risen Christ. There is no psychological basis for believing that this many people over this long a period of time (40 days), including skeptics, would all have been hallucinating.

Finally, the hallucination theory does not explain the empty tomb. There was no hallucinating the empty tomb. There is nothing that can reveal the paucity of a hallucination better than hard contrary evidence. In short, there is no evidence of any kind which supports the fanciful hallucination theory as a viable alternative to the resurrection of Jesus Christ.

No One Mistakenly Misidentified Jesus Christ

Hugh J. Schonfield (*The Passover Plot*) tries to say that the disciples and others mistook other individuals for the risen Christ. He would have us believe that the disciples wanted so much to see Jesus that they went around the landscape pointing out anyone as Jesus "risen from the grave."

However, this theory completely ignores the primary evidence. One look at Jesus' body, still in the grave, would have shocked the disciples out of their silly misidentification habit. But the grave was empty. Schonfield neglects to discuss the appearances of Christ where clear identification was made (John 20; Luke 24). He rejects without warrant or evidence the highly credible evidence of 1 Corinthians 15:6 that over

500 people at one time saw and later attested to the risen Christ. His whole thesis is without historical, textual, or psychological support.

Christ's Character Is Consistent with His Resurrection

Once the Gospel record has been shown to be reliable, there is no real basis left for an attack upon Christ's character. The verdict of Pilate at the trial of Jesus Christ has been the conclusion of history: "I find no guilt in this man" (Luke 23:4).

Anyone who rejects the resurrection of Jesus Christ assails his character and ethics. Jesus said repeatedly that he was going to die and rise again (John 2:19-21). He referred to his own impending death on numerous occasions throughout his ministry (Matthew 12:40; 16:21; Luke 9:22; John 10:17,18). Even after his resurrection, Jesus referred to his death and resurrection (Luke 24:20-27). He reminded the incredulous disciples after his resurrection that he had told them before his death that he would "suffer and rise again from the dead" (Luke 24:46).

Those who did not know Jesus Christ personally said, "How can a man who is a sinner perform such signs?" (John 9:16). The unbelieving soldier at the crucifixion cried out, "Truly this man was the son of God!" (Mark 15:39).

Those who knew Jesus best had even higher praise for him. Peter said, "Thou art the Christ, the Son of the living God" (Matthew 16:16). The apostles and their associates said of his character:

> He knew no sin (2 Corinthians 5:21).
> He was without sin (Hebrews 4:15).
> He was an unblemished and spotless lamb (1 Peter 1:19).
> In him there is no darkness at all (1 John 1:5).
> He committed no sin, nor was any deceit found in his mouth (1 Peter 2:22).

What a testimony to his impeccable character by people who were his contemporaries!

Most nonchristians do not share the antagonism concerning Christ's character which we reviewed in the first part of this chapter. The antichristian philosopher John Stuart Mill, quoted earlier, wrote of Christ:

> About the life and sayings of Jesus there is a stamp of personal originality combined with profundity of insight, which [place him] in the very first rank of men of sublime genius of whom our species can boast. When this preeminent genius is combined with the qualities of probably the greatest moral reformer and martyr to that mission who ever existed upon earth, religion cannot be said to have made a bad choice in pitching upon this man as the ideal representative and guide of humanity.[35]

Even the American Unitarian writer Channing, who denied the deity of Christ, acknowledged Christ's unblemished character in these words:

> This form of benevolence, the most disinterested and divine form, was, as you well know, manifested by Jesus Christ in infinite strength, amidst injuries and indignities which cannot be surpassed.... I cannot enlarge on other traits of the character of Christ. I will only observe that it had one distinction which more than anything forms a perfect character.[36]

W. E. H. Lecky, the eminent British historian of the last century, depicted the character of Christ in these words:

> The character of Jesus has not only been the highest pattern of virtue, but the strongest incentive to its practice, and has exerted so deep an influence,

that it may be truly said, that the simple record of three short years of active life has done more to regenerate and to soften mankind, than all the disquisitions of philosophers and than all the exhortations of moralists.[37]

The famous French deist Renan summed it up well when he said of Jesus, "His beauty is eternal, and his reign shall never end. Jesus is in every respect unique, and nothing can be compared with him."[38]

Conclusion

The atheistic attacks on the person and works of Jesus Christ are futile. For every atheistic attack there is a sound response from history, evidence, and reason. The Jesus Christ of Christian faith is not the Jesus Christ of the skeptic. The Jesus Christ of the skeptic is fiction. The Jesus Christ of Christian faith is fact.

CHAPTER 7

Pantheism Attacks Christ

Pantheism makes many assertions about Jesus Christ which are also made by atheism. Both deny the deity of Christ. Both deny his death on the cross for our sins (the atonement) and his resurrection from the dead as described in the Bible. Both deny supernaturalism (the atheists because there is no God at all, and the pantheist because God is the universe, and thus his acts cannot be from outside the natural). But pantheism also makes unique assertions concerning the person and work of Christ which need to be dealt with separately from the attacks of atheism.

Occult Magician?

Pantheists believe that Jesus was a master occult magician who had unusual powers (psychic powers) by virtue of being indwelt by the "Christ spirit," or some sort of realization or practice of the pantheistic divinity. The pantheist cannot take the message of the New Testament at face value, but must either deny its authority or arbitrarily reinterpret it. There is almost universal agreement among pantheists that Jesus of Nazareth, who was most certainly not God himself (but "divine" in the sense that all of existence is divine), lived, performed unusual feats, died, and reappeared. (The differences in pantheistic interpretation of his being, life, and character will be discussed as necessary below.) Let us examine first the pantheistic attack on Jesus Christ's being.

Deity Under Attack

Foremost among the attacks of pantheism on Jesus Christ is the attack on his deity. The great Indian leader Mahatma Gandhi, a Hindu pantheist, said, "I regard Jesus Christ as one of the greatest teachers of mankind, but I do not consider him to be the 'only Son of God.' Many passages in the Bible are mystical.* For me 'the letter killeth, the spirit giveth life.' "[1]

The founder of the American religious cult Christian Science, Mary Baker Eddy, insisted that "Jesus Christ is not God, as Jesus himself declared...."[2] Benjamin Creme, one of the New Age "prophets," said flatly, "The Christ is not God."[3] In Levi's *Aquarian Gospel,* reviewed at more length earlier in this book, is a story which recounts that a woman who knelt to worship Christ was rebuked by him with these words: "Good woman, stay; take heed to what you do; you may not worship man, this is idolatry."[4]

Although it may sound contradictory of a Christian unfamiliar with reinterpretation of terms, pantheists do believe that Christ is divine. As Creme put it, Christ is "a divine man, but divine in exactly the sense that we are divine."[5] Acclaimed actress, reincarnationist, and pantheist Shirley MacLaine said bluntly, "You are God. You know you are Divine."[6] She said earlier in her book that the only real difference between Christ and us is that "he was a highly evolved spiritual soul whose purpose on earth was to impart the teachings of a Higher Order."[7]

---

* Pantheism continually hints at redefinition of terms as an escape from the clear teachings of Scripture.

Christhood Under Attack

Most pantheists make a strange dichotomy between the man Jesus of Nazareth and "the Christ," which they reinterpret in a mystical way. They do not believe that Jesus of Nazareth was the Christ. They believe that the divine Christ spirit or power or divinity dwelt in the early Jesus. Benjamin Creme and many other pantheists believe that the Christ spirit came upon Jesus at his baptism. Creme personalizes this Christ spirit:

> The body was that of Jesus. From the Baptism onwards, sometimes Jesus Himself was in it; sometimes Jesus and the Christ used it simultaneously; while at still other times the Christ alone manifested through it.[8]

Another New Age writer, David Spangler, has a similar view of "Jesus" and "the Christ":

> Jesus, building on the foundation of revelation of the past, brought forth within his own being the birth of the Christ. [By doing this] he made of his individual soul and body a perfect instrument through which the wholeness of the Christ consciousness could demonstrate.[9]

Theosophy, one of the first contemporary pantheistic cults, affirms that "the Christ" is not something unique to Jesus, but is instead the divine principle in all of us. The *Theosophical Glossary* notes, "Every good individual, therefore, may find Christ in his 'inner man' as Paul expresses it...whether he be Jew...Hindu, or Christian."[10]

Mark L. Prophet, the late founder of the pantheistic cult called the Church Universal and Triumphant, clearly divided the Christ from Jesus:

Let not the term "Christ" be a stumbling block
to your evolution. Understand that this word has
been misused in its application to only one son of
God when it should have been the acknowledged
birthright of every son and daughter in all ages. For
did not this Christ declare through Jesus, "Before
Abraham was, I AM"?[11]

Pantheists, then, deny the unique deity of Jesus Christ,
substituting instead a "Christ" deity which any individual does
or should possess.

The Christ Spirit

Pantheists believe that the "Christ spirit" indwelt Jesus and
is somehow accessible to all of us. They tend to be universalis-
tic: They believe that since everything is somehow part of God,
every belief, religion, and religious name is somehow part of
the divine whole. They think of Christ, for example, as just
one name of the divine power available to humans. Benjamin
Creme says:

He is known in the East by other names: as the
Lord Maitreya to the Buddhists, as the Bodhisattva
to the Hindus, the Iman Mahdi to the Moslems, the
Messiah to the Jews.[12]

Just who is this occult master who is called the Christ and
many other names? He is a divine force or energy. Pantheists
may differ on exactly how they describe this force, but they
agree that he (it?) is a force. New Age writer David Spangler
explains the "Christ force" in contrast to the "Lucifer* force"
this way:

Christ is the same force as Lucifer but moving in

---

* Although the name is the same, New Age thinkers do not acknowledge this one as the Lucifer (Satan) of the Bible.

seemingly the opposite direction Lucifer moves in to create the light within through the pressure of experience. Christ moves out to release that light, that wisdom, that love into creation so what has been forged in the furnace of creation can become a light unto the world and not simply stagnate within the being.[13]

Spangler's Christ, like his Lucifer, is neither good nor bad. They are simply opposite poles, two sides of the same coin, the yin and the yang of Buddhism, two aspects of the same force. Like the light side and the dark side of the Force in *Star Wars,* we can use these energies, says Spangler, for good or evil.

Manifestations of God

Many pantheists, especially those who look to Hinduism or Buddhism for their teachings, believe that the impersonal and all-encompassing pantheistic God has, at various times, incarnated himself into a personal manifestation through a master or teacher or guru. These gurus teach their followers (devotees) the shortest "path" to realizing and experiencing their own intrinsic and pantheistic divinity.

Pantheists like this usually call Jesus Christ only one of the several manifestations of the deity. The devotees of the Indian guru Maharaj Ji chant daily, "I bow before my Guru, who is greater than Christ or Buddha, for each of them was the servant of this Satguru."[14]

Another well-known guru is Sai Baba. When a cynical reporter, now a devotee, asked a follower of Sai Baba, "Who is this sorcerer?" the follower replied, "Don't talk like that! Say sorry. He is God."[15] Sai Baba is not shy to claim the same divine status for himself accorded him by his devotees. He said, "I am God. My power is divine and has no limit. There is no force natural or supernatural that can stop me and my mission."[16]

One way that pantheists can deny the unique deity of Jesus

Christ is to give other persons the same divinity or even more divinity. Like Sai Baba, Jesus Christ was a guru who showed his devotees the path to realizing their own divinity!

Miracles Under Attack

Pantheists deny that Jesus Christ performed miracles (defined as supernatural acts) because they deny the existence of anything supernatural. Remember that for the pantheists God is the universe, so his acts or "miracles" cannot originate from outside the universe. How do pantheists explain Jesus' miracles? By simply redefining the term "miracle," making it to mean a psychic act, hypothetically possible by anyone. Jesus was more adept at using the "cosmic force," "divine energies," "force," etc., than are most men. The so-called miracles he performed are no different from the feats by other gurus and occult masters.

According to Benjamin Creme, "These miracles are now being performed by men and women in the world all the time."[17] These supernormal (but not supernatural) talents include telepathy, clairvoyance, ESP, and healings. The *Theosophical Glossary* says that "miracle" is a misnomer for magic, which is defined as—

> the power of man by magic practices to command the services of the gods: which gods, are in truth, but the occult powers or potencies of Nature, personified by the learned priests themselves, in which they reverenced only the attributes of the one unknown and nameless Principle.... Magic is the science of communicating with and directing supernal, supramundane Potencies, as well as of commanding those of the lower spheres; a practical knowledge of the hidden mysteries of nature known to only the few, because they are so difficult to acquire, without falling into sins against nature.[18]

Some pantheists will distinguish among the miracles reported in Jesus' ministry, rejecting some as impossible and accepting others as evidence of "natural " powers. Gandhi wrote:

> There is no miracle in the story of the multitude being fed on a handful of loaves. A magician* can create that illusion. But woe wroth the day on which a magician would be hailed as the Savior of humanity. As for Jesus raising the dead to life, well, I doubt if the men he raised were really dead.[19]

Resurrection Under Attack

An essential element in most pantheistic systems is the belief in reincarnation. Reincarnation is the belief that at death a person's spirit or soul is "born" into a new body for a new life. (A similar belief is transmigration, which says that the soul can be "born" into other forms of life, from human to animal, etc.) Reincarnation is part of the common pantheistic salvation plan, where one settles the "karmic debt" of his past negative deeds through successive incarnations. Most pantheists substitute reincarnation for the biblical concept of resurrection. If pantheists use the word "resurrection," they usually redefine it to mean reincarnation, or perhaps absorption into the Divine Mind, or passing from one level of occultic awareness to another, etc. How do pantheists escape the New Testament teaching concerning the bodily resurrection of Jesus Christ from the dead?

Some pantheists refuse to admit that Jesus Christ really died on the cross. Mary Baker Eddy, founder of Christian Science (one of the few pantheistic groups which does not believe in reincarnation), said:

> His disciples believed Jesus to be dead while

---

* "Magic" variously refers to sleight-of-hand showmanship or to the practice of occult or psychic phenomena.

he was hidden in the sepulchre, whereas he was
alive, demonstrating within the narrow tomb the
power of Spirit to overrule mortal, material
sense....[The resurrection of Jesus] was a method
of [spiritual] surgery beyond material art, but it was
not a supernatural act...it was a divinely natural
act.[20]

Other pantheists say that Jesus did not die on the cross
because all death is an illusion. Christ merely sloughed off his
mortal body to enjoy the freedom of pure spirit. *The Aquarian
Gospel* says, "Jesus did not sleep within the tomb. The body
is the manifest of soul; but the soul is soul without its manifest
[body]."[21] Mark L. Prophet of the Church Universal and
Triumphant asserts that anything which is real cannot die:

That which is real, that which is born of God,
created in the image and likeness of the flame of Life
itself, cannot die. For the laws of disintegration and
death do not apply to that perfect creation which
God hath made.
Only that which is unreal can die. And in this
context we define death as the cessation of being.[22]

This kind of "death and resurrection" is nothing more than
the soul surviving death and being prepared for incarnation
into another body (reincarnation). According to these pantheists, Jesus did not return to his physical body. No one ever
does. He, and everyone else, comes into a new body.
Some other pantheists come up with even more speculative
explanations for the biblical account of the resurrection of Jesus
Christ. Anglican archdeacon Michael Perry proposes the novel
idea that Jesus' resurrection was a combination of the hallucination theory and mental telepathy. The postresurrection
appearances of Christ were telepathic visions of the dead.
Unlike "ordinary" hallucination, one needs to be in no special
emotional state to experience this. Perry's theory, discussed

in his book *The Easter Enigma,* is that when Jesus rose in the "spiritual body," he sent telepathic communications to his disciples. These telepathic communications "triggered" resurrection hallucinations in the disciples.[23]

A Christian Response to Pantheism

Pantheism denies that Jesus of Nazareth was the Christ, truly God and truly man, that he died physically on the cross, and that he came back to life in his material, physical, and glorified body. We will evaluate those denials below.

The New Testament Record Is Trustworthy

Pantheists are generally less sophisticated in their attacks on the trustworthiness of the New Testament record than are atheists. Rather than concentrating on an evidential or literary attack on the New Testament, pantheists usually escape the record through two means: 1) assuming that much of the "gospel" was lost, destroyed, and/or changed (the assumption behind *The Aquarian Gospel*); and 2) reinterpreting anything in the New Testament record which contradicts their own beliefs (as in Mary Baker Eddy's *Science and Health with Key to the Scriptures*).

However, the response presented in the last chapter is more than sufficient to answer the pantheists' arguments. The New Testament we have today is an accurate, clear record of what the eyewitnesses recorded concerning the person and work of Jesus Christ. We can trust the New Testament to tell us the truth.

In contrast to the attack by some critics of Christ, the New Testament teaches clearly that Jesus claimed to be God, claimed to be uniquely the Christ, the only Son of God the Father, actually died, and actually rose bodily from the grave.

Jesus Claimed to Be Christ

Jesus said clearly many times that he was the predicted Old

Testament Messiah (Greek equivalent, Christ). He told the woman of Samaria, who asked if he was the "Messiah to come," "I who speak to you am He" (John 4:26). When the high priest asked Jesus at his trial if he was the Christ, he answered, "I am; and you shall see the Son of Man sitting at the right hand of Power, and coming with the clouds of heaven" (Mark 14:62; cf. Daniel 7:13,14).

The terms "Messiah" and "Christ" as applied to Jesus in the Bible were never understood in some generic sense, referring to someone other than the unique Son of God. Throughout the New Testament we find affirmation that Jesus is the Christ, the unique Son of God. Matthew 1:17 refers to him as "the Christ," not *a* Christ. Far from becoming the Christ at his baptism, the New Testament teaches clearly that Jesus was the Christ from his birth. When the angel announced the birth of Jesus to the shepherds he identified Jesus this way: "Today in the town of David a Savior has been born to you; *he is Christ the Lord*" (Luke 2:11 NIV). The righteous and devout Simeon, who was at the Jerusalem temple when the infant Jesus was circumcised, supernaturally recognized his Savior, fulfilling God's promise to him that "he would not die before he had seen the Lord's Christ" (Luke 2:26 NIV).

There is no distinction between Jesus and the Christ. Jesus is the Christ. In fact, the Bible strongly denounces those who deny that Jesus is the Christ: "Who is the liar? It is the man who denies that Jesus is the Christ. Such a man is the antichrist—he denies the Father and the Son" (1 John 2:22 NIV).

Earlier we showed conclusively from the New Testament that Jesus claimed to be God and that the New Testament asserted that he was and is God. There are other ways to show from the Bible that Jesus Christ is God.

Jesus Accepted Worship As God

Jesus was a Jew. Jews were forbidden to worship anyone or anything but God (Exodus 20:4,5; Deuteronomy 6:4,5,13).

Jesus affirmed this, the first and greatest of all the command-
ments, many times in his teachings (Matthew 4:10; etc.). But
Jesus allowed numerous people to bow down and worship him.
The magi "fell down and worshiped Him" (Matthew 2:11).
One of the lepers healed by Jesus worshiped him Matthew 8:2).
A blind man whom Jesus healed said to him, " 'Lord, I
believe.' And he worshiped Him" (John 9:38). When Jesus
appeared to his disciples in Galilee after his resurrection
Matthew says, "When they saw Him they worshiped Him"
(Matthew 28:17). God the Father himself commanded all the
angels to worship Jesus (Hebrews 1:1-8).

Jesus Is Identified with Jehovah

The following chart summarizes some of the New Testament
identifications of Jesus with Jehovah in the Old Testament.

Jehovah	Title or Act	Jesus
Isaiah 40:28	Creator	John 1:3
Isaiah 45:22; 43:11	Savior of souls	John 4:42
1 Samuel 2:6	Raise dead	John 5:21
Joel 3:12; Matthew 25:31	Judge of souls	John 5:27; cf.
Isaiah 60:19,20	The true Light	John 8:12
Exodus 3:14; John 18:5,6	I AM	John 8:58; cf.
Psalm 23:1	Spiritual Shepherd	John 10:11
Isaiah 42:8; cf. Isaiah 48:11	Glory of God	John 17:1,5
Isaiah 41:4; 44:6	First and Last	Revelation 2:8
Hosea 13:14	Redeemer	Revelation 5:9
Isaiah 62:5 Hosea 2:16	Bridegroom	Revelation 21:2; cf. Matthew 25:1ff.
Psalm 18:2	Rock	1 Corinthians 10:4
Jeremiah 31:34	Forgiver of sins	Mark 2:7,10
Psalm 148:2	Worshiped by angels	Hebrews 1:6

| Psalm 148:5 | Creator of angels | Colossians 1:16 |
| Isaiah 45:23 | Confessed as Lord | Philippians 2:9-11 |

Jesus Did What Only God Can Do

According to the Bible, God alone was the Creator of all things (Isaiah 44:24; Hebrews 3:4). However, the Bible also declares that Jesus Christ created all things (John 1:3; Colossians 1:15-17).

According to the Bible, God alone can forgive sin (Isaiah 44:21,22; Mark 2:7,10). But the Bible also declares the Jesus Christ can forgive sin (Matthew 9:6).

According to the Bible, God alone has the power within himself to raise the dead (1 Corinthians 6:14). But the Bible also declares that Jesus Christ can raise the dead (John 5:27-29).

According to the Bible, God the Father raised Jesus Christ from the dead (Acts 2:24). But the Bible also says Jesus Christ raised himself from the dead (John 2:19-21; 10:18). (The third member of the Trinity, the Holy Spirit, also raised Christ from the dead, according to Romans 8:11.)

From the above and the section in Chapter 6 on the deity of Christ, it is abundantly clear that Jesus Christ is uniquely God.

Jesus Rose Bodily from the Dead

Not only did Jesus Christ claim to be God, but he offered his bodily resurrection from the dead as a unique proof of his claim (Matthew 12:38-40; 16:21). The New Testament evidence for the bodily resurrection of Jesus Christ is overwhelming.

Let us first define what we mean by "resurrection." The biblical concept of resurrection should not be confused with reincarnation, resuscitation, or the simple existence of the soul after the death of the body. Resurrection means the changing of one's natural, material body (the only one he has) from mortal to immortal, from earthly to heavenly, from perishable to imperishable, from weak to powerful, from corruptible to incorruptible, and from natural to supernatural (see especially 1 Corinthians 15:40-53).

Jesus Christ was resurrected, not reincarnated. He had the same body, but glorified, which he possessed before his death (Luke 24:39; John 20:26-29). Jesus Christ was resurrected, not resuscitated. His glorified body would never die again (Revelation 1:18), unlike the resuscitated bodies of Lazarus and other people whom Jesus raised from the dead. Jesus Christ was resurrected, not separated from his body. His resurrection was material, not spirit (Luke 24:39).

There is both abundant and high-quality testimony from contemporaries of Jesus Christ who were eyewitnesses of his resurrection. Within the first century after Christ's resurrection, while the contemporaries of Christ were still alive, there are at least seven separate and independent records of his resurrection. The testimonies are found in Matthew 28, Mark 16, Luke 24, John 20 and 21, 1 Corinthians 15, Hebrews 1 and 2, and 1 Peter 3. Of these accounts, four were written by apostles of Christ (Matthew, John, 1 Corinthians, 1 Peter). One (Mark) was written by an associate of the apostle Peter, and another (Luke) was written by an associate of the apostle Paul. The one unknown writer (Hebrews) speaks of being a contemporary of the apostles (Hebrews 2:3,4) and a coworker with Timothy, who was Paul's missionary companion (Hebrews 13:23).

In brief, there is no other record of any event in the ancient world which enjoys the quantity and quality of attestation which the resurrection of Jesus Christ enjoys.

The resurrection witnesses of Jesus Christ were many. Jesus was seen by more than 500 people after his resurrection. Among these to whom Jesus appeared were women, relatives, disciples, and even outsiders (Luke 24). Jesus appeared to a doubter (Thomas in John 20) and to two unbelievers (James and Paul). On one occasion Jesus appeared to 500 people at the same time (1 Corinthians 15:6). This instance was recorded by the apostle Paul only 22 years after the resurrection (55 A.D.). Paul added a significant test about the witness of the 500: Most of them were still alive at the time Paul was writing. William Lillie noted:

> What gives a special authority to the list as historical evidence is the reference to most of the five hundred brethren being still alive. St. Paul says in effect, "If you do not believe me, you can ask them." Such a statement in an admittedly genuine letter written within thirty years of the event is almost as strong evidence as one could hope to get for something that happened nearly two thousand years ago.[24]

Jesus also appeared in his resurrected body many times during the 40 days after the resurrection. At least ten such occasions are listed in the New Testament:

1. To Mary Magdalene (John 20:11).
2. To other women (Matthew 28:9,10).
3. To Peter (Luke 24:34).
4. To two disciples (Luke 24:13-32).
5. To ten apostles (Luke 24:33-39).
6. To Thomas and the ten apostles (John 20:26-29).
7. To seven apostles (John 21).
8. To all the apostles (Matthew 28:16-20).
9. To 500 brethren (1 Corinthians 15:6).
10. To James (1 Corinthians 15:7).

These ten appearances were at different times and different places, to different people, over a period of 40 days (Acts 1:3). During this time Jesus revealed his wounds to them, taught them, ate with them, and performed miracles before them. This kind of evidence places the recognition of his true identity and his bodily resurrection from the dead beyond question.

All four Gospels record that the tomb in which Jesus' dead body was laid was empty. His physical body was permanently gone from there. Add to the empty tomb Jesus' numerous bodily appearances, and the fact of the bodily resurrection is inescapable.

Jesus revealed his "flesh and bones" to skeptical disciples as proof of his resurrection from the dead (Luke 24:39; John 20:26-30). In Luke 24:39 Jesus said, "Touch Me and see, for a spirit does not have flesh and bones as you see that I have." Jesus denied that he was merely a spirit or immaterial entity.

Twice the New Testament records Jesus showing his crucifixion wounds after his resurrection to convince the disciples that he had really risen. In the first passage Jesus said, "See My hands and My feet, that it is I myself" (Luke 24:39). In the second passage Jesus challenged doubting Thomas to test his resurrection, saying, "Reach here your finger, and see My hands; and reach here your hand, and put it into My side; and be not unbelieving, but believing" (John 20:27). That the resurrection body showed the scars of the crucifixion proves that it was the same body which had been crucified and had died.

Jesus also proved that he had a resurrected body by eating and drinking with the disciples after his resurrection (Acts 10:41). First Jesus ate supper with the two Emmaus Road disciples (Luke 24:30). Then he ate with the other disciples (Luke 24:42,43). The third time Jesus cooked breakfast by the Sea of Galilee with seven disciples (John 21:9-15). Eating and drinking is another evidence of the literal, physical nature of Jesus' resurrected body.

There were evidently many other ways in which Jesus proved to his followers that he had risen bodily from the grave. Acts 1:3 NIV tells us, "After his suffering, he showed himself to these men and gave many convincing proofs that he was alive" (cf. John 20:30). We have no record now identifying these other proofs, but the caliber of the proofs we do possess compels us to accept the bodily resurrection of Jesus Christ from the grave. The sum total of this evidence is an overwhelming testimony to the physical, bodily resurrection of Jesus Christ.

Any pantheistic (or, for that matter, atheistic) attack on the resurrection of Jesus Christ does an injustice to the historical, primary source documents, and is completely unreasonable. For example, the "telepathic hallucination" theory ignores the empty tomb, makes Jesus morally culpable for deceiving his disciples, ignores ordinary psychological assumptions, and stretches our credibility beyond reason concerning the numerous people and times involved in the resurrection appearance accounts. There is no biblical, factual, moral, or psychological basis for believing this or any other theory which denies the bodily resurrection of Jesus Christ.

Conclusion

The most amazing power of Christ's resurrection is not his ability to eat fish or appear in a closed room. It is not his ability to be caught up into heaven in the sight of the disciples. The most amazing power of Christ's resurrection is that it is the seal of his sacrifice of our sins, the promise which empowers the transformation of individuals from skeptics to believers.

One such skeptic began ten years of research of the resurrection of Christ with this assumption:

> When, as a young man, I first began seriously to study the life of Christ, I did so with a very definite feeling that, if I may so put it, his history rested on very insecure foundations.... [My purpose] was to take this last phase of the life of Jesus...to strip it of its overgrowth of primitive beliefs and dogmatic suppositions, and to see this supremely great person as he really was.[25]

However, ten years of researching the evidence forced Frank Morison to believe in the bodily resurrection of Jesus Christ from the dead, and his story is told in his now-classic *Who Moved the Stone?* in which he concluded:

> There may be, and, as the writer thinks, there certainly is, a deep and profoundly historical basis

for that much disputed sentence in the apostles'
creed—"the third day he rose again from the
dead."[26]

Frank Morison is not the only skeptic who has embraced
the faith of Jesus Christ after being confronted with the reality
of the resurrection of Jesus Christ. The famous German scholar
Wolfhart Paanenberg noted:

> The resurrection of Jesus acquires such decisive
> meaning, not merely because someone or any one
> has been raised from the dead, but because it is Jesus
> of Nazareth, whose execution was instigated by the
> Jews because he had blasphemed against God. If this
> man was raised from the dead, then that plainly
> means that the God whom he had supposedly
> blasphemed has committed himself to him.[27]

But simply accepting the historicity of the resurrection is no
guarantee of Christian conversion or allegiance to the religious
claims of Jesus Christ. Rabbi Pinchas Lapide is convinced that
the resurrection actually happened.[28] He rejects Jesus' claims,
nonetheless, refusing to admit that he is the promised Jewish
Messiah. A letter to the editor in *Time* magazine concerning
Rabbi Lapide makes a telling blow against Lapide's inconsistent
view:

> Pinchas Lapide's logic escapes me. He believes it
> is a possibility that Jesus was resurrected by God.
> At the same time he does not accept Jesus as the
> Messiah. But Jesus said that he was the Messiah.
> Why would God resurrect a liar?[29]

Whether atheists, pantheists, skeptics, or fence-straddlers
like Lapide, the evidence is there for all of them to see if they
are willing to examine it and then act reasonably on the facts
they find. The New Testament documents are historical,

primary source documents, and they provide abundant proof for the person and work of Jesus Christ. But the One they uplift offers more than simple history. Jesus said, "You diligently study the Scriptures because you think that by them you possess eternal life. These are the Scriptures that testify about me, yet you refuse to come to me to have life" (John 5:39,40 NIV). It is only from Jesus Christ himself that the individual can be transformed from death into life and be assured of that resurrection power in his own life. Believing in, trusting in, putting oneself into the hands of Jesus Christ is the only way to obtain that abundant life which God incarnate has promised to those who love him: "These are written that you may believe that Jesus is the Christ, the Son of God, and that by believing you may have life in his name" (John 20:31 NIV).

CHAPTER 8

God and Christ Victorious

Atheism and pantheism have become tools for Satan in his relentless attack upon the Christian church. The power of pseudointellectualism, the seduction of pseudospirituality, and the fury of Satan's rage combine to batter Christ and his church.

But God's Word, the Bible, tells us that God and Christ are victorious: Satan will not win. Atheism is nothing more than pseudointellectualism: It is not reasonable, logical, or true. On the contrary, God is worshiped through truth (John 4:24), and Jesus Christ declared, "I am the way, and the truth, and the life" (John 14:6). Pantheism is nothing more than pseudospirituality, substituting contradictory and empty mysticism for the spiritual life possible only through Christ. God is the source of our spiritual life, as Christ declared: "If any man is thirsty, let him come to Me and drink. He who believes in Me, as the Scripture said, 'From his innermost being shall flow rivers of living water' " (John 7:37,38).

We have seen in this book that atheism and pantheism have nothing real to offer the person searching for meaning, purpose, and truth in life. Atheism and pantheism have claimed to be what they are not: reality. Atheism seeks to chew up

Christianity and spit it out. Pantheism seeks to chew up Christianity and swallow it. Neither one can ultimately triumph.

The Church Under Siege

In Chapter 1 we saw the enormous power and popularity wielded by atheism and pantheism in contemporary American society. We saw how atheism has quietly infiltrated our major social structures, including politics, education, and even religion. We saw how secular humanism cannot be compatible with Christianity. We saw how secular humanism cannot even tolerate Christianity. In fact, secular humanists believe that they have a duty to "liberate" mankind from Christianity.

In Chapter 1 we also saw how pantheism has swept through our American society, sometimes in the guise of fads, sometimes in the bold costumes of "scientific principles" or "wholistic living." We saw how pantheism, by making everything God, actually degrades God and makes him nothing of value.

Pantheism and atheism have even affected our morals. Both remove any objective, absolute values or ethics from our world, reducing us and our actions to biochemical reactions (materialistic atheism) or karmic destiny (pantheism).

False Gods of Our Times

In Chapter 2 we discussed the seven major world views regarding God. We used our "flow chart" of beliefs to outline the different ideas that people can have about God. Everybody has some kind of idea about God; even if a person is not sure what he believes, that uncertainty is an opinion in itself. First of all, a person either believes in some sort of god or he does not (*atheism*).

If one believes in some sort of god(s), he either believes in may gods (*polytheism*) or else he believes in just one god. If he believes in only one god, then he either identifies that god with the universe (*pantheism*) or else he believes that his god is somehow essentially distinct from the universe. The pantheist, for example, would not agree that God created the universe out of nothing, but instead out of himself. A significant variation from pantheism is *panentheism*, which identifies God with the universe in a very close but slightly differentiated way, somewhat like the relationship in man between his body and his soul. If one believes that God is distinct in essence from the universe, then he either believes that this God is finite, (*finite godism*) or else he believes that God is infinite. If one believes that God is infinite, then he believes that God does or does not act in his creation, the universe. The belief that God does not act in his universe is called *deism*. Some of the founding fathers of the United States were deists. The deist denies all miracles. The belief in one God, distinct from his universe and infinite, who does act in the universe, is called *theism*. Christians (and Jews and Muslims) are theists.

Our survey in Chapter 2 showed us that none of these seven views of God fits reality and reason except for Christian theism. All gods except for the Christian God are false gods of our times.

Atheism Attacks God

In Chapter 3 we saw the various forms of attack used by atheism against Christianity. We saw the difference between atheism, which asserts that there is no God, and *agnosticism,* which says that a person does not or cannot know whether God exists. Atheism is not passive: It is an active and dynamic belief which attacks Christian theism. This attack has been carried on by every atheist of renown throughout the centuries.

We also looked at some of the ways in which atheists have attacked Christian theism. We saw that atheists misunderstand what theists mean when they say "God is the uncaused Cause." Atheists also don't have any substantial arguments against the theistic assertion that the universe is finite and must have been caused and is sustained by something infinite outside the universe: God. We saw how science, far from denying the

Christian God, supports theism when it is stripped of its antitheistic and antisupernaturalistic presuppositions. Finally, Chapter 3 also showed us the bankrupt condition of atheistic ethics and the inability of atheism to argue against Christianity on the basis of ethics. Atheism does not result from any lack of evidence that God is there, but rather from a willful rejection of the abundant evidence that God *is* there.

Pantheism Attacks God

Chapter 4 surveyed the most common assertions of pantheism against the Christian God. Although pantheists often say that their beliefs can encompass and complement Christian belief, such is not the case. There is no compatibility between pantheism and Christian theism. Theism says that God is beyond the universe. Pantheism says that God is the universe.

Theism says that God is distinct from the universe. Pantheism says that God is the same as the universe.

Theism says that God made the universe out of nothing. Pantheism says that God made the universe out of himself.

Theism says that God created all that is. Pantheism says that God is all that is.

Theism says that the supernatural is beyond the natural. Pantheism says that the supernatural is within the natural.

Theism says that the universe had a beginning. Pantheism says that the universe is eternal.

Theism says that man is like God. Pantheism says that man is God.

Theism says that God is to the universe like a painter is to his painting. Pantheism says that God is to the universe as the ocean is to water drops in it.

In surveying pantheistic thought, we saw that pantheism is inadequate as a world view in a number of different ways. Pantheism is not rational, its claims are self-defeating, it cannot be proved, its view of God is inconsistent, it has no adequate explanation for human error, it cannot explain evil adequately, it destroys the distinction between good and evil, and it encourages indifference to human suffering.

Pantheism fails to usurp Christianity. Like atheism, pantheism cannot provide an adequate world view. It must be abandoned for the reasonableness and truth of Christian theism.

Naturalism Attacks Miracles

Chapter 5 showed us the atheistic and pantheistic attacks on miracles and gave a strong Christian defense of the supernatural: the miraculous intervention of the Almighty Creator, God, into this universe which is his creation.

Miracles are not optional to Christian belief: They are *integral* to Christian belief. If there are no miracles, there is no resurrection. If there is no resurrection, then Christ is not resurrected, and he is not God. As the apostle Paul put it so eloquently:

> If Christ has not been raised, your faith is worthless; you are still in your sins. Then those also who have fallen asleep in Christ have perished. If we have hoped in Christ in this life only, we are of all men most to be pitied (1 Corinthians 15:17-19).

Christian miracles are testable, both with the mind and with the evidence. Christianity, including the cornerstone miracle, the resurrection of Jesus Christ, is testable history which proves our claims as Christians.

After we surveyed the history of naturalism and looked at the assertions of the most significant spokesmen against miracles, we answered the main challenges against miracles. We noted that, if a person can be convinced of the existence of God, then the existence of miracles follows naturally and logically. We saw that the true relationship between pantheism, natural law, and miracles exposes pantheism as viewing miracles from a twisted perspective, and that Christian theism sees correctly that miracles are interventions from the Creator.

As Christians we do not deny the supernormal, but we view and judge it from the basis of Christian theism, not from atheism or pantheism. Biblical miracles are far superior to occult magic and to the fraudulent occult tricks often foisted upon the unwary as "evidence" of the psychic realm. Chapter 5 showed us that Christian theism with its miracles, epitomized by the resurrection of Jesus Christ, is the ultimate testimony to the superiority of supernaturalism over naturalism.

Atheism Attacks Christ

In Chapter 6 we surveyed the atheistic attacks against the person and work of Jesus Christ. We compared and contrasted the biblical, testable view of Jesus Christ with the spurious suppositions of atheists about Jesus Christ. Atheists affirm, against the evidence, that Jesus Christ is not historical. Some atheists refer to him as mythical. Some atheists deny that Jesus Christ died on the cross, thereby hoping to escape the reality of his resurrection from the dead. All atheists deny that Jesus Christ rose from the dead, giving a variety of inadequate guesses to try to account for the overwhelming evidence of the resurrection's reality. In response, we showed that the New Testament documents are historically reliable. They tell us the truth about Christ and his death and resurrection. We saw that Christ was not mythologized, that he did die on the cross, and that he did rise miraculously from the dead. The Jesus Christ of Scripture is the Jesus Christ of fact.

Pantheism Attacks Christ

Finally, in Chapter 7, we saw how pantheism attacks the person and work of Jesus Christ. Some pantheists see Christ as an occult magician. Some see him as divine only in some limited sense as all of us are divine, part of the all-encompassing God. Pantheists directly contradict the Bible by refusing to acknowledge Jesus as the Christ. They do not believe that Jesus Christ is unique. Pantheists attack the bodily resurrection of

Jesus Christ, referring instead to reincarnation or absorption into the divine mind. We also saw how the Christian faith can meet and refute every challenge sent forth from the pantheists concerning Jesus Christ.

Conclusion

We have seen throughout the pages of this book that Christianity is superior to any other belief system. God and Christ are victorious: Truth is in Jesus Christ, not in any man-made system of atheism or pantheism. I leave you with the words of the apostle Peter, who pledged his life to upholding the truth of Christianity:

> We did not follow cleverly invented stories when we told you about the power and coming of our Lord Jesus Christ, but we were eyewitnesses of His majesty.... And we have the word of the prophets made more certain, and you will do well to pay attention to it, as to a light shining in a dark place, until the day dawns and the morning star rises in your hearts (2 Peter 1:16,19 NASB, NIV).

NOTES

CHAPTER 1

1. "Competency and Controversy," in *Skeptical Inquirer*, vol. 8, Fall 1983, p. 2.
2. *Atheists United: An Introduction* (Los Angeles: Atheists United, 1983), p. 4.
3. Paul Kurtz, ed., *Humanist Manifesto I and II* (Buffalo: Prometheus Books, 1973), p. 10.
4. *Atheists United Newsletter* (Los Angeles: Atheists United, 1984), pp. 3, 7-8.
5. Bhagwan Shree Rajneesh, *The Mustard Seed*, comp. Swami Amrit Pathik, ed. Swami Satyan Deva (San Francisco: Harper and Row, 1975), p. 400.
6. Dean C. Halverson, "Escape...The Orange Way," in *Spiritual Counterfeits Newsletter*, vol. 8, no. 2, Feb.-Mar. 1982, p. 2.
7. William Greene, *est: 4 Days to Make Your Life Work* (New York: Simon and Schuster, 1976), p. 131.
8. Association for Research and Enlightenment, *A Search for God, Book I* (Virginia Beach: A.R.E., 1969), p. 115.

CHAPTER 2

1. Billy Graham, *How to Be Born Again* (Waco: Word Books, 1977), pp. 29-30.
2. C. S. Lewis, *Mere Christianity* (New York: The Macmillan Company, 1943), p. 44.
3. C. S. Lewis, *Miracles* (New York: The Macmillan Company, 1947), pp. 30-31.
4. C. S. Lewis, *Mere Christianity*, p. 73.
5. Carl Sagan, *Cosmos* (New York: Random House, 1980), p. 345.
6. Ibid., p. 243.
7. Ibid., p. 4.
8. Charles Darwin, *Origins* 3rd ed., "Introduction."
9. Ayn Rand, *The Virtue of Selfishness* (New York: New American Library, 1961), p. 15.

10. Paul Kurtz, *The Humanist Manifesto* (Buffalo: Prometheus Books, 1973), p. 8.
11. Ibid.
12. Ibid., p. 1.
13. Ibid., p. 13.
14. Ludwig Feuerbach, *The Essence of Christianity* (New York: Harper Torchbooks, 1957), p. 14.
15. Karl Marx and Friedrich Engels, *On Religion* (New York: Schocken Books, 1964), p. 50.
16. Erich Fromm, *Psychoanalysis and Religion* (London: Yale University Press, 1950, 1967), p. 49.
17. Ayn Rand, *For the New Intellectual* (New York: New American Library, 1961), p. 65.
18. Sigmund Freud, *The Future of an Illusion* (Garden City: Doubleday & Company, Inc., 1964), pp. 52-53.
19. Jean-Paul Sartre, *Existentialism and Humanism* (London: Methuen & Co., Ltd., 1948), p.34.
20. *Star Wars*, p. 81.
21. Ibid., p. 120.
22. *Time*, May 23, 1983.
23. *Rolling Stone*, July 24, 1980, p. 37.
24. Benjamin Creme, *Reappearance*, p. 115.
25. Shirley MacLaine, *Out on a Limb*, p. 347.
26. Alfred North Whitehead, *Religion in the Making* (New York: Meridian Books, 1967), pp. 150-51.
27. Alfred North Whitehead, *Process and Reality* (New York: Harper Torchbooks, 1960), p. 521.
28. Charles Hartshorne, *A Natural Theology for Our Times* (LaSalle: The Open Court Publishing Company, 1967), pp. 113-14.
29. Harold S. Kushner, *When Bad Things Happen to Good People* (New York: Avon Books, 1981).
30. John Stuart Mill, *Three Essays on Religion* (London: Longmans, Green and Company, 1885), p. 30.
31. Peter Bertocci, *Introduction to Philosophy of Religion* (New York: Prentice Hall, Inc., 1953), p. 398.
32. Henry Wilder Foote, *Thomas Jefferson* (Boston: The Beacon Press, 1947), p. 49.
33. Thomas Jefferson, *The Jefferson Bible*, "Introduction," pp. vii-viii.

34. Calvin Blanchard, ed., *The Complete Works of Thomas Paine* (Chicago: Belford, Clarke & Co., 1885), p. 150.
35. Treaty between the United States of America and Tripoli, 1796.
36. David L. Miller, *The New Polytheism: Rebirth of the Gods and Goddesses* (New York: Harper and Row, 1974), p. 4.
37. Ibid., pp. 76-77.
38. Ibid., pp. 80-81.
39. Walter Martin, *The Maze of Mormonism* (Ventura: Vision House Publishers, 1978), pp. 74-75.
40. Joseph Smith, Jr., *History of the Church of Jesus Christ of Latter-day Saints* (Salt Lake City: Deseret Book Company, 1976), 6:305-6.
41. Ibid., 6:475-76.
42. Brigham Young, *Journal of Discourses* (Salt Lake City: Deseret Book Company, n.d.), 7:333.

CHAPTER 3

1. Bertrand Russell, "What Is an Agnostic?" in *Look*, 1953.
2. Karl Marx, *Marx*, p. 295.
3. Gary DeYoung letter, Feb. 14, 1964.
4. George Smith, Atheism: The Case Against God (Buffalo: Prometheus Press, 1975), p. xi.
5. Friedrich Nietzsche, *The Portable Nietzsche*, p. 627.
6. Thomas Altizer, *Radical Theology*, p. 47.
7. Ayn Rand, *For the New Intellectual* (New York: New American Library, 1961), p. 151.
8. Carl Sagan, *The Edge of Forever*, p. 257.
9. Anonymous, "American Atheists: Aims and Purposes," in *The American Atheist*, vol. 19, no. 5, inside front cover.
10. Gordon Stein, *How to Argue with a Theist (and Win)* (Culver City, CA: The Free Thought Association, 1979), p. 2.
11. Carl Sagan, *Edge*, p. 257.
12. Robert Jastrow, *God and the Astronomers* (New York: W. W. Norton and Company, Inc., 1978), pp. 114-15.
13. Ibid., p. 111.
14. Kenny, *Five Ways*, p. 66.
15. Dagobert D. Runes, *Dictionary of Philosophy* (Totowa, NJ: Littlefield, Adams and Company, 1977), p. 4.
16. Ibid., p. 97.

17. Richard Purtill, *Reason to Believe* (Grand Rapids: William B. Eerdmans Publishing Company, 1974), pp. 83-84.
18. J. Y. T. Greig, ed., *The Letters of David Hume* (2 vols.) (Oxford: Clarendon Press, 1932), 1:187.
19. David Hume, *Enquiry Concerning Human Understanding* (Indianapolis: Bobbs-Merrill, 1955), pp. 165-66.
20. Wald, "Origin," p. 48.
21. Fred Hoyle, *Evolution*, pp. 24, 148.
22. Russell F. Doolittle, "Probability and the Origin of Life," in *Scientists Confront Creationism*, Laurie R. Godfrey, ed. (New York: W. W. Norton and Company, 1983), p. 96.
23. Carl Sagan, *Cosmos* (New York: Random House, 1980), p. 278.
24. Carl Sagan, *Broca's Brain* (New York: Random House, 1979), p. 275.
25. Herbert Yockey, "Self Organization, Origin of Life Scenarios and Information Theory," in *The Journal of Theoretical Biology*, vol. 91 (1981): 13-31.
26. Thaxton, *Mystery*, p. 186.
27. David Hume, *Dialogues Concerning Natural Religion* (Indianapolis: Bobbs-Merrill, 1962), p. 66.
28. Kushner, *Bad Things*.
29. Lewis, *Miracles*.
30. Nietzsche, *Portable*, p. 627.
31. Jean-Paul Sartre, *Words*, p. 102.
32. Ibid., pp. 252-53.
33. Thomas Molnar, "Jean-Paul Sartre, RIP," in *National Review*, June 11, 1982, p. 677.

CHAPTER 4

1. Rajneesh, *Mustard Seed*, p. 264.
2. Ibid., p. 400.
3. Benjamin Creme, *Reappearance of the Christ and the Masters of Wisdom* (Los Angeles: Tara Press, 1980), p. 47.
4. Alice Bailey, *The Reappearance of the Christ* (New York: Lucis Publishing Company), p. 140.
5. *Golden Book of the Theosophical Society* (Los Angeles: The Theosophy Company, 1925), pp. 63-64.
6. Alice Bailey, *The Externalization of the Hierarchy* (New York: Lucis Publishing Company), p. 551.

7. "Levi," Levi H. Dowling, *The Aquarian Gospel of Jesus the Christ* (Santa Monica: DeVorss & Co., Publishers, 1907 and 1964), p. 16.

8. Ibid., p. 249 (168:1-2).

9. Geoffrey Parrinder, *A Dictionary of Non-Christian Religions* (Philadelphia: The Westminster Press, 1971), p. 280.

10. Johannes Aagaard, "Modern Syncretist Movements—A General Overview," in *New Religious Movements Up-Date*, Mark Albrechts, ed. (Arhus, Denmark: The Dialogue Center, vol. 5, no. 2, Aug. 1981), p. 29.

11. Creme, *Reappearance*, p. 111.

12. David Spangler, *Revelation: The Birth of a New Age* (San Francisco: The Rainbow Bridge, 1976), p. 60.

13. Prabhavananda, *Spiritual Heritage*, p. 45.

14. Spangler, *Revelation*, p. 221.

15. Shirley MacLaine, *Out on a Limb* (New York: Bantam Books, 1983), p. 325.

16. *Time*, May 23, 1983, p. 68.

17. Bailey, *Reappearance*, p. 144.

18. James Kahn, *Return of the Jedi*, based on a story by George Lucas (New York: Ballantine Books, 1983), p. 138.

19. Dale Pollock, *Skywalking: The Life and Films of George Lucas* (New York: Harmony Books, 1983), p. xvi.

20. T. D. Suzuki, *Introduction to Zen Buddhism*, pp. 46, 38.

21. Mary Baker Eddy, *Science and Health with Key to the Scriptures* (Boston: The Christian Science Publishing Society, 1973), 583:24-25; 113:16-18.

22. Levi, *Aquarian Gospel*, 22:12-15.

23. Ibid., p. 18.

24. Marilyn Ferguson, *The Aquarian Conspiracy* (Los Angeles: J. P. Tarcher, Inc., 1980), p. 382.

25. MacLaine, *Limb*, p. 268.

26. Eddy, *Science and Health*, 113:19-20.

27. Ibid., 584:9-11.

28. Ibid., 588:1.

29. Ibid., 584:17-18.

30. Helena P. Blavatsky, *Theosophical Glossary* (Los Angeles: The Theosophy Company, 1973), p. 139.

31. Alan Watts, *The Way of Zen* (New York: Random House, 1957), p. 20.

32. Plotinus, *The Enneads*, Stephen MacKenna, trans. (London: Faber and Faber Limited, 1966), VI, pp. 4, 16.
33. Levi, *Aquarian Gospel*, 17:7.
34. Creme, *Reappearance*, p. 123.
35. Watts, *Zen*, p. 52.
36. Ayn Rand, *For the New Intellectual* (New York: New American Library, 1961), p. 12.
37. Alan Watts, *Myth and Ritual in Christianity* (London: Thames & Hudson, 1964), p. 21.
38. Lewis, *Miracles*, p. 29.
39. Mark Twain, *Christian Science* (New York: Harper & Brothers Publishers, n.d.), p. 38.
40. Francis Schaeffer, *The God Who Is There* (Downers Grove: InterVarsity Press, 1968), p. 101.

CHAPTER 5

1. Benedict de Spinoza, *A Theologico-Political Treatise and A Political Treatise* (New York: Dover Publications, Inc., 1951), p. 83.
2. David Hume, *An Inquiry Concerning Human Understanding* (New York: The Bobbs-Merrill Company, Inc., 1955).
3. Immanuel Kant, *Religion Within the Limits of Reason Alone* (New York: Harper and Row, 1960), p. 84.
4. John Dewey, *A Common Faith* (New Haven: Yale University Press, 1934), pp. 46, 71.
5. Julian Huxley, *Religion Without Revelation* (New York: New American Library, 1957), pp. 187, 62.
6. George Smith, *Atheism: The Case Against God* (Los Angeles: Nash Publishing, 1974), p. 233.
7. Hobbes, *Leviathan*, 1:8:70.
8. Spinoza, *Treatise*, p. 83.
9. Ibid., p. 85.
10. Ibid., p. 89.
11. Ibid., p. 90.
12. Hume, *Inquiry*, 10:1:122-23.
13. Bertrand Russell, *The Basic Writings of Bertrand Russell*, Robert Egner and Lester Denonn, eds. (New York: Simon and Schuster, 1961), p. 62.
14. Carl Sagan, *Broca's Brain* (New York: Random House, 1979), p. 130.

15. Lewis, *Miracles*, p. 105.
16. Richard Whately, *Doubts*, p. 290.
17. Robert Jastrow, *God and the Astronomers* (New York: W. W. Norton and Company, 1979), pp. 114-15.
18. Ibid., pp. 115-16.
19. D. M. Armstrong, *A Theory of Universals*, vol. 2 (Cambridge: Cambridge University Press, 1978), p. 156.
20. Levi, *Aquarian Gospel*, 37:12.
21. Eddy, *Science and Health*, 591:21-22.
22. Ibid., 139:4-5.
23. Levi, *Aquarian Gospel*, 23:5-6.
24. Eddy, *Science and Health*, 44:20-27.
25. Marilyn Ferguson, *The Aquarian Conspiracy* (Los Angeles: J. P. Tarcher, Inc., 1980), p. 182.
26. Alice Bailey, *Externalization*, pp. 508-9.
27. Fritjof Capra, *The Tao of Physics* (New York: Bantam Books, 1984), p. 117.
28. Benjamin Creme, *The Reappearance of the Christ* (Los Angeles: Tara Center, 1980), p. 46.
29. Bailey, *Externalization*, p. 403.
30. Creme, *Reappearance*, p. 136.
31. *New Science*, Oct. 17, 1974, p. 174.
32. Ibid., p. 175.
33. Ibid., p. 185.
34. *Nature*, Oct. 18, 1974, p. 55.
35. *New Science*, op. cit., p. 174.
36. Uri Geller, *My Story* (New York: Praeger Publishers, 1975), p. 216.
37. Ruth Montgomery, *A Gift of Prophecy* (New York: William Morrow & Company, 1965), p. viii.
38. Ibid., p. 15.

CHAPTER 6

1. Russell, *Writings*, p. 593.
2. Albert Schweitzer, *The Quest of the Historical Jesus* (New York: The Macmillan Company, 1948), p. 398.
3. Calvin Blanchard, ed., *The Complete Works of Thomas Paine* (Chicago: Belford, Clarke & Company, 1885), p. 234.
4. John H. Randall, *Hellenistic Ways of Deliverance and the Making of the Christian Synthesis* (1970), p. 154.

5. Hugh J. Schonfield, *Those Incredible Christians*, 1968, p. xii.
6. Abdullah Yusuf Ali, *The Meaning of the Glorious Quran*, vol. 1, 4:157.
7. B. C. Johnson, *The Atheist Debater's Handbook* (Buffalo: Prometheus Books, 1981), p. 121.
8. Kirsopp Lake, *The Historical Evidence for the Resurrection of Jesus Christ* (London: Williams & Norgate, 1907), pp. 247-79.
9. Hugh J. Schonfield, *The Passover Plot* (Bernard Geis Associates, 1965), p. 152.
10. Friedrich Nietzsche, *Portable*, p. 601.
11. Russell, *Writings*, p. 593.
12. Ibid., p. 594.
13. Schonfield, *Plot*, p. 41.
14. Ibid., p. 185.
15. John A. T. Robinson, *Redating the New Testament* (Philadelphia: The Westminster Press, 1976), p. 352.
16. Ibid., p. 360.
17. William F. Albright in *Christianity Today*, Jan. 1963, p. 359.
18. Nelson Glueck, *Rivers in the Desert* (New York: Farrar, Strauss & Cudahy, 1959), p. 136.
19. Sir William Ramsay, *St. Paul the Traveller and the Roman Citizen* (Grand Rapids: Baker Book House, 1949), p. 8.
20. Millar F. Burrows, *What Mean These Stones?* (New Haven: American Schools of Oriental Research, 1941), p. 1.
21. Glueck, *Rivers*.
22. Tacitus, *Annals*, 10:44.
23. Tacitus, *Arabian Antiquities*, 18:33.
24. Seutonius, *The Life of Claudius*, 25:4.
25. Pliny, *Epistles*, 10:96.
26. Sanhedrin 43a, "Eve of Passover," in *Babylonian Talmud*.
27. Justin Martyr, *Apology*, 1:48.
28. A. E. Sherwin-White, *Roman Society and Roman Law in the New Testament* (Grand Rapids: Baker Book House, 1963), pp. 188-91.
29. Ibid., p. 190.
30. Julius Muller, *The Theory of Myths, in its Application to the Gospel History, Examined and Confuted* (London: John Chapman, 1844), p. 26.
31. Will Durant, *The Story of Civilization*, 3:557.

32. William F. Albright, *The Scrolls and Christianity* (1969), p. 57.
33. Cook, ed., *Commentary*, pp. 349-50.
34. Ibid.
35. Vernon C. Grounds, *The Reason for Our Hope* (Chicago: Moody Press, 1945), p. 34.
36. William Ellery Channing, *Unitarian Christianity and Other Essays* (New York: The Bobbs-Merrill Company, Inc., 1957), p. 76.
37. W. E. H. Lecky, *History of European Morals from Augustus to Charlemagne* (2 vols.) (London: Longmans, Green, and Company, 1869), 2:88.
38. Frank Mead, ed., *The Encyclopedia of Religious Quotations* (Westwood, NJ: Fleming H. Revell, n.d.), p. 57.

CHAPTER 7

1. Mohatmas Gandhi, *The Message of Jesus Christ* (Bombay: Bharatiya Vidya Bhavan, 1963), p. 41.
2. Mary Baker Eddy, *Message* (Boston: Christian Science Publishing Society, 1901), 8:10-11.
3. Creme, *Reappearance*, p. 115.
4. Levi, *Aquarian Gospel*, p. 36.
5. Creme, *Reappearance*, p. 120.
6. MacLaine, *Limb*, p. 209.
7. Ibid., p. 91.
8. Creme, *Reappearance*, p. 54.
9. David Spangler, *Reflections on the Christ* (Scotland: Findhorn Foundation, 1978), p. 27.
10. Helena Petrovna Blavatsky, *The Theosophical Glossary* (Los Angeles: The Theosophical Company, 1973), p. 84.
11. Mark L. Prophet, *Cosmic Consciousness* (Los Angeles: Summit University Press, 1981), p. 56.
12. Creme, *Reappearance*, p. 73.
13. Spangler, *Reflections*, p. 40.
14. Guru Maharaj Ji, *The Glory of the Guru* (Boulder, CO: The Divine Light Mission, n.d.), p. 2.
15. Raman, *Illustrated Weekly of India*, Mar. 15, 1981, p. 37.
16. Ibid.
17. Creme, *Reappearance*, p. 146.
18. Blavatsky, *Glossary*, p. 197.
19. Gandhi, *Message*, p. 73.

20. Eddy, *Science and Health*, 44:22-24.
21. Levi, *Aquarian Gospel*, 172:15.
22. Prophet, *Consciousness*, p. 40.
23. Michael Perry, *The Easter Enigma*, pp. 141-95.
24. William Lillie, "The Empty Tomb and the Resurrection," in *Historicity and Chronology in the New Testament*, by D. E. Nicham (1965), p. 125.
25. Frank Morison, *Who Moved the Stone?* (Grand Rapids: Zondervan Publishing House, 1978), pp. 9-11.
26. Ibid., p. 193.
27. William Lane Craig, *The Son Rises* (Chicago: Moody Press, 1981), p. 141.
28. *Christianity Today*, Mar. 2, 1984. See also Pinchas Lapide, *The Resurrection of Jesus: A Jewish Perspective* (Minneapolis: Augsburg Publishing House, 1983).
29. *Time*, June 4, 1979.

GLOSSARY OF TERMS

Page numbers refer to the first time the entry appears in the text. (q.v.—the preceding term is defined elsewhere in the glossary.)

A

Aagaard, Professor Dr. Johannes—contemporary European Christian cult apologist (q.v.)............................... 68

Accidental—in philosophy (q.v.), an attribute of something that is not necessary to that thing............................ 46

ACLU—American Civil Liberties Union.................. 8

Adonis—Greek god of mythology.......................121

Agnosticism—literally means "without knowledge," and refers in this context to the belief that one does not or cannot know if God exists... 40

Akashic Records—the universal psychic (q.v.) mind of pantheism (q.v.), referred to as the source of the pseudo-revelation the *Aquarian Gospel of Jesus the Christ* (q.v.).............. 66

Albright, William F.—one of the most famous biblical archaeologists (q.v.) whose many finds gave much support to the historical accuracy of the Bible.................................133

Altizer, Thomas J. J.—philosopher and popularizer of the "God is dead" movement................................... 41

American Atheists—contemporary atheist (q.v.) organization founded and headed by atheist Madalyn Murray O'Hair (q.v.).

Analogy—correspondence in some respects between things otherwise different... 48

Anselm, St.—of Canterbury, 1033-1109. Christian philosopher most noted for his ontological argument to prove God's existence... 21

Apocryphal gospels—writings of the second and third centuries which claimed to be gospels about Jesus Christ; pseudo-gospels...138

Apologetics—in this study, that branch of theology (q.v.) which states the reasons for accepting the Christian world view. It means giving a defense for what one believes................. 4

Aquarian Conspiracy, The—popular sociological book assessing the New Age Movement (q.v.) from a secular (q.v.) standpoint, by Marilyn Ferguson (q.v.)............................... 77

C

God's will pervades human and cosmic events, and that man is utterly dependent upon God 21

Can We Trust the New Testament?—popular contemporary book by liberal Anglican bishop John A. T. Robinson (q.v.) re-evaluating and supporting the idea that the New Testament books were written soon after the events they describe 131

Capra, Fritjof—contemporary author whose *The Tao of Physics* (q.v.) seeks to reconcile Eastern pantheism (q.v.) with western physics 104

Cayce, Edgar—founder of the Association for Research and Enlightenment (q.v.) who gave medical "readings" and religious revelations while he was in a trance. Known as "the sleeping prophet" 12

Chalcedon Creed—fifth-century affirmation and summation of the central doctrines of the Christian biblical faith, as recognized by an ecumenical church council 118

Christian Science—modern pantheistic cult founded by Mary Baker Eddy (q.v.) denies the reality of sin, sickness, and death, and denies the unique deity of Jesus Christ 27

Church of Jesus Christ of Latter-day Saints (Mormons)—the name of the religious cult founded in 1830 by Joseph Smith, Jr. (q.v.), commonly known as the Mormons (q.v.), denying biblical authority and doctrine, espousing polytheism (q.v.) 35

Church Universal and Triumphant, The—Eastern pantheistic (q.v.) cult founded by Mark L. Prophet (q.v.) 151

Clairvoyance—an occultic (q.v.) practice or ability of seeing objects or persons psychically (q.v.) 104

Cobb, John—American panentheistic (q.v.) theologian 29

Commun(ist)(ism)—(Marxist) political and philosophical system which presupposes that creating the perfect society (through violent revolution) will perfect mankind morally, emotionally, and socially 7

Cosmic—in this context, used especially by Eastern and New Age proponents to describe something related to the pantheistic (q.v.) god.

Cosmic humanism—man is the measure of all things because of his identity with the divine cosmos 28

Cosmos—reference to the universe; also the name of the popular television series hosted by astronomer and secular humanist (q.v.) Carl Sagan (q.v.) 23

E

Easter Enigma, The—book by Anglican archdeacon Michael Perry (q.v.), discounting the resurrection of Jesus Christ 157

Eclectic—choosing or consisting of what appears to be the best from diverse sources 68

Eddy, Mary Baker—founder of the American pantheistic cult called Christian Science (q.v.) 65

Enlightenment—used in a mystical context to refer to an altered (and presumably higher) state of spiritual or psychic awareness ... 9

Erhard, Werner—founder of Erhard Seminars Training (est) (q.v.), now known as The Forum 12

Erhard Seminars Training (est)—now called The Forum, cult founded by Werner Erhard as a nonreligious self-help program based on the presupposition that each person is his own god and can solve his problems through divine action 10

ESP—abbreviation for extra-sensory perception, a term referring to the supposed psychic (q.v.) ability to discern or know things by supernormal means 104

Essence—in this context, what makes a thing what it is, and not something else 18

Essential—in philosophy, the attributes which make a thing what it is, and not something else; its essential attributes are necessary to its being 46

est—abbreviation for Erhard Seminars Training (q.v.) 10

Eternal—when referring to the biblical God, that which has no beginning or ending, as in God's existence; in other contexts, that which has no (discernible) ending (e.g., Christians have "eternal" life, but were created at a point in time) 22

Ethics—moral philosophy, the study which concerns itself with judgment of right and wrong, good and bad, etc. 26

Ethical Culture—catchall term used by the United States Supreme Court to describe an ethical system which is based on the society or culture around it rather than on something objective and absolute 17

F

Fakers, The—Christian book by a Christian magician, Danny Korem (q.v.), and a Christian physician which exposes the fraudulent practices of occultists (q.v.) 109

Kurtz, Paul—philosopher, atheist, and leader of the secular humanist (q.v.) movement in the United States.................... 25

Kushner, Rabbi Harold S.—contemporary Jewish author who promotes finite godism (q.v.)......................... 32

L

Lapide, Rabbi Pinchas—contemporary Jewish rabbi who admits the reality of the resurrection of Jesus Christ but denies the deity of Christ 165

Lake, Kirsopp—liberal theologian (q.v.) who denies the bodily resurrection of Jesus Christ............................... 125

Lamaas—one of the characters in Levi H. Dowling's (q.v.) pseudo-revelation, the *Aquarian Gospel of Jesus the Christ* (q.v.).. 76

Levi—common name of Levi H. Dowling (q.v.), author of New Age (q.v.) pseudo-revelation scripture of Jesus Christ called the *Aquarian Gospel of Jesus the Christ* (q.v.).................... 64

Lewis, C. S.—20th century Christian author, scholar, and professor of literature...................................... 21

Literary (higher) criticism—the technique of investigating and explaining the Bible through examining the words, grammar, and syntax of the text..................................... 131

Lucas, George—filmmaker and originator of the popular "Star Wars" (q.v.) movie saga........................... 28

Lucifer—biblically refers to the archangel who later fell from grace through rebellion against God and is now Satan, the Devil; many New Age Movement groups use the term to refer to the principle of light which enables them to understand the mysteries of the universe.. 106

Luther, Martin—1483-1546. Beginner of the Protestant Reformation (q.v.), founder of the Lutheran church(es).......... 21

M

McDowell, Josh—Christian apologist (q.v.)............... 122

MacLaine, Shirley—award-winning actress and author who espouses pantheism and reincarnation.......................... 28

Magic—variously refers to sleight-of-hand showmanship or to the practice of occultic (q.v.) or psychic (q.v.) phenomena.. 154

Magician—one who practices magic (q.v.).

195

FURTHER READING

Ali, Abdullah Yusuf. *The Meaning of the Glorious Quran*. New York: New York Press, n.d.

Altizer, Thomas. *Radical Theology*. Indianapolis: Bobbs-Merrill, 1960.

Armstrong, D.M. *A Theory of Universals*. Cambridge: Cambridge University Press, 1978.

Bailey, Alice. *The Externalization of the Hierarchy*. New York: Lucis Publishing Company, n.d.

Bailey, Alice. *The Reappearance of the Christ*. New York: Lucis Publishing Company, n.d.

Bertocci, Peter. *Introduction to Philosophy of Religion*. New York: Prentice Hall, Inc., 1953.

Blanchard, Calvin, ed. *The Complete Works of Thomas Paine*. Chicago: Belford, Clarke & Co., 1885.

Blavatsky, Helena P. *Theosophical Glossary*. Los Angeles: The Theosophy Company, 1973.

Burrows, Millar F. *What Mean These Stones?* New Haven: American Schools of Oriental Research, 1941.

Capra, Fritjof. *The Tao of Physics*. New York: Bantam Books, 1984.

Channing, William Ellery. *Unitarian Christianity and Other Essays*. New York: The Bobbs-Merrill Company, Inc., 1957.

Craig, William Lane. *The Son Rises*. Chicago: Moody Press, 1981.

Creme, Benjamin. *The Reappearance of the Christ and the Masters of Wisdom*. Los Angeles: Tara Center Press, 1980.

Dewey, John. *A Common Faith*. New Haven: Yale University Press, 1934.

Dowling, Levi H. ("Levi"). *The Aquarian Gospel of Jesus the Christ*. Santa Monica: DeVorss & Co., Publishers, 1907, 1964.

Eddy, Mary Baker. *Science and Health with Key to the Scriptures*. Boston: The Christian Science Publishing Society, 1973.

Ferguson, Marilyn. *The Aquarian Conspiracy*. Los Angeles: J. P. Tarcher, Inc., 1980.

Feuerbach, Ludwig. *The Essence of Christianity*. New York: Harper Torchbooks, 1957.

Foote, Henry Wilder. *Thomas Jefferson*. Boston: The Beacon Press, 1947.

Freud, Sigmund. *The Future of an Illusion*. Garden City: Doubleday & Company, Inc., 1964.

Fromm, Erich. *Psychoanalysis and Religion*. London: Yale University Press, 1950, 1967.

Gandhi, Mohatmas. *The Message of Jesus Christ*. Bombay: Bharatiya Vidya Bhavan, 1963.

Geller, Uri. *My Story*. New York: Praeger Publishers, 1975.

Glueck, Nelson. *Rivers in the Desert*. New York: Farrar, Strauss & Cudahy, 1959.

Godfrey, Laurie R., ed. *Scientists Confront Creationism*. New York: W. W. Norton and Company, 1983.

Graham, Billy. *How to Be Born Again*. Waco: Word Books, 1977.

Greene, William. *est: 4 days to Make Your Life Work*. New York: Simon and Schuster, 1976.

Grounds, Vernon C. *The Reason for Our Hope*. Chicago: Moody Press, 1945.

Hartshorne, Charles. *A Natural Theology for Our Times*. La Salle: The Open Court Publishing Company, 1967.

Hobbes, Thomas. *Leviathan*. New York: Bobbs-Merrill, 1958.

Hoyle, Fred, and N. C. Wickramasinghe. *Evolution from Space*. New York: Dent, n.d.

Hume, David. *Dialogues Concerning Natural Religion*. Indianapolis: Bobbs-Merrill, 1962.

Hume, David. *An Inquiry Concerning Human Understanding*. New York: Bobbs-Merrill Company, 1955.

Hume, David. *The Letters of David Hume*. J. Y. T. Greig, ed. Oxford: Clarendon Press, 1932.

Huxley, Julian. *Religion without Revelation*. New York: New American Library, 1957.

Jastrow, Robert. *God and the Astronomers*. New York: W. W. Norton and Company, Inc., 1978.

Ji, Guru Maharaj. *The Glory of the Guru*. Boulder, CO: The Divine Light Mission, n.d.

Johnson, B.C. *The Atheist Debater's Handbook*. Buffalo: Prometheus Books, 1981.

Kahn, James. *Return of the Jedi*. Based on a story by George Lucas. New York: Ballantine Books, 1983.

Kant, Immanuel. *Religion Within the Limits of Reason Alone*. New York: Harper and Row, 1960.

Kenny, Anthony. *Five Ways: St. Thomas Aquinas' Proofs of God's Existence*. Notre Dame, IN: University of Notre Dame Press, 1980.

Kurtz, Paul, ed. *Humanist Manifestos I and II*. Buffalo: Prometheus Books, 1973.

Kushner, Harold S. *When Bad Things Happen to Good People*. New York: Avon Books, 1981.

Lake, Kirsopp. *The Historical Evidence for the Resurrection of Jesus Christ*. London: Williams and Norgate, 1907.

Lecky, W. E. H. *History of European Morals from Augustus to Charlemagne*. London: Longmans, Green and Company, 1869.

Lewis, C. S. *Mere Christianity*. New York: The Macmillan Company, 1943.

Lewis, C. S. *Miracles*. New York: The Macmillan Company, 1947.

Lucas, George. *Star Wars: From the Adventures of Luke Skywalker*. New York: Ballantine Books, 1976.

MacLaine, Shirley. *Out on a Limb*. New York: Bantam Books, 1983.

Martin, Walter. *The Maze of Mormonism*. Ventura, CA: Vision House Publishers, 1978.

Marx, Karl. *Marx*. Peter Singer, ed. London: Oxford University Press, 1980.

Marx, Karl, and Friedrich Engels. *On Religion*. New York: Schocken Books, 1964.

Mead, Frank, ed. *The Encyclopedia of Religious Quotations*. Westwood, NJ: Fleming H. Revell, n.d.

Mill, John Stuart. *Three Essays on Religion*. London: Longmans, Green and Company, 1885.

Miller, David. *The New Polytheism: Rebirth of the Gods and Goddesses*. New York: Harper and Row, 1974.

Montgomery, Ruth. *The Gift of Prophecy*. New York: William Morrow & Company, 1965.

Morison, Frank. *Who Moved the Stone?* Grand Rapids: Zondervan Publishing House, 1978.

Muller, Julius. *The Theory of Myths, in Its Application to the Gospel History, Examined and Confuted*. London: John Chapman, 1844.

Nietzsche, Friedrich. *The Portable Nietzsche*. Walter Kaufman, ed. New York: Viking Portable Library, 1977.

Parrinder, Geoffrey. *A Dictionary of Non-Christian Religions*. Philadelphia: The Westminster Press, 1971.

Pollock, Dale. *Skywalking: The Life and Films of George Lucas*. New York: Harmony Books, 1983.

Prabhavananda. *Spiritual Heritage of India.* Hollywood: Vedanta Press, 1979.

Prophet, Mark L. *Cosmic Consciousness.* Los Angeles: Summit University Press, 1981.

Purtill, Richard. *Reason to Believe.* Grand Rapids: William B. Eerdmans Publishing Company, 1974.

Rajneesh, Bhagwan Shree. *The Mustard Seed.* Comp. Swami Amrit Pathik. Ed. Swami Satyan Deva. San Francisco: Harper and Row, 1975.

Ramsay, Sir William. *St. Paul the Traveller and the Roman Citizen.* Grand Rapids: Baker Book House, 1949.

Rand, Ayn. *For the New Intellectual.* New York: New American Library, 1961.

Rand, Ayn. *The Virtue of Selfishness.* New York: New American Library, 1961.

Randall, John H. *Hellenistic Ways of Deliverance and the Making of the Christian Synthesis.* New York: Columbia University Press, 1970.

Robinson, John A. T. *Redating the New Testament.* Philadelphia: The Westminster Press, 1976.

Runes, Dagobert D. *Dictionary of Philosophy.* Totowa, NJ: Littlefield, Adams and Company, 1977.

Russell, Bertrand. *The Basic Writings of Bertrand Russell.* Robert Egner and Lester Denonn, eds. New York: Simon and Schuster, 1961.

Sagan, Carl. *Broca's Brain.* New York: Random House, 1979.

Sagan, Carl. *Cosmos.* New York: Random House, 1980.

Sartre, Jean-Paul. *Existentialism and Humanism.* London: Methuen & Co., Ltd., 1948.

Sartre, Jean-Paul. *Words.* New York: George Braziller, 1964.

Schaeffer, Francis. *The God Who Is There.* Downers Grove: InterVarsity Press, 1968.

Schonfield, Hugh J. *The Passover Plot.* New York: Random House, 1965.

Schonfield, Hugh J. *Those Incredible Christians.* London: Hutchinson Publishers, 1968.

Schweitzer, Albert. *The Quest of the Historical Jesus.* New York: The Macmillan Company, 1948.

Sherwin-White, A. E. *Roman Society and Roman Law in the New Testament.* Grand Rapids: Baker Book House, 1963.

Smith, George. *Atheism: The Case Against God.* Buffalo: Prometheus Press, 1975.

Smith, Joseph, Jr. *History of the Church of Jesus Christ of Latter-day Saints.* Salt Lake City: Deseret Book Company, 1976.

Spangler, David. *Reflections on the Christ.* Scotland: Findhorn Foundation, 1978.

Spangler, David. *Revelation: The Birth of a New Age.* San Francisco: The Rainbow Bridge, 1976.

Spinoza, Benedict de. *A Theologico-Political Treatise and A Political Treatise.* New York: Dover Publications, Inc., 1951.

Suzuki, T. D. *Introduction to Zen Buddhism.* New York: Grove Press, 1964.

Thaxton, Charles B., Walter L. Bradley, and Roger L. Olsen. *The Mystery of Life's Origin: Reassessing Current Theories.* New York: Philosophical Library, 1984.

Twain, Mark. *Christian Science.* New York: Harper and Brothers, Publishers, n.d.

Watts, Alan. *Myth and Ritual in Christianity.* London: Thames and Hudson, 1964.

Watts, Alan. *The Way of Zen.* New York: Random House, 1957.

Whately, Richard. *Historical Doubts Relative to Napolean Buonaparte.* London: A. J. Valpy and Company, 2nd ed., 1821.

Whitehead, Alfred North. *Religion in the Making.* New York: Meridian Books, 1967.

Young, Brigham. *Journal of Discourses.* Salt Lake City: Deseret Book Company, n.d.

Now See the Exciting New Film